JULIAN BENNETT

TOWNS IN ROMAN BRITAIN

Third edition

SHIRE ARCHAEOLOGY

Cover photographs
(Top left) The Newport Arch at Lincoln. The only surviving Roman gateway in Britain, it
was originally built in the second century to mark the north entrance to the *Colonia*
(Domitiana) Lindenensis. (Cadbury Lamb)
(Bottom left) The Old Work at Wroxeter, part of the Roman *thermae*: the wall originally
divided the *palaestra* from the *tepidarium* with its hypocaust, visible
in the foreground. (Charles Daniels)
(Right) The Roman wall at *Verulamium* built in the third century of local stone with tile
bonding courses. (Cadbury Lamb)

British Library Cataloguing in Publication Data:
Bennett, Julian
Towns in Roman Britain. – 3rd ed.
– (Shire archaeology; 13)
1. Cities and towns, Ancient – Great Britain
2. Great Britain – Antiquities, Roman
I. Title
936.1'009732
ISBN 0 7478 0473 7

Published in 2001 by
SHIRE PUBLICATIONS LTD
Cromwell House, Church Street, Princes Risborough,
Buckinghamshire HP27 9AA, UK.
(Website: www.shirebooks.co.uk)

Series Editor: James Dyer.

Number 13 in the Shire Archaeology series.

ISBN 0 7478 0473 7

First published 1980. Second edition 1984; reprinted 1988. Third edition 2001.

Printed in Great Britain by
CIT Printing Services Ltd, Press Buildings,
Merlins Bridge, Haverfordwest, Pembrokeshire SA61 1XF.

Contents

LIST OF ILLUSTRATIONS 4

PREFACE AND ACKNOWLEDGEMENTS 5

1. THE URBANISATION OF BRITAIN 7

2. PUBLIC BUILDINGS AND AMENITIES 17

3. HOUSING AND HOUSEHOLDS 29

4. WEALTH, COMMERCE AND INDUSTRY 38

5. RELIGION AND RELIGIOUS BUILDINGS 47

6. URBAN SOCIETY IN ROMAN BRITAIN 56

7. CHANGE AND TRANSFORMATION 64

8. FURTHER READING 74

9. SITES AND MUSEUMS TO VISIT 76

10. ROMAN NAMES OF SOME PLACES MENTIONED IN THE TEXT 78

INDEX 79

4

List of illustrations

Figure 1. Comparative sizes of some walled towns in Roman Britain *page 6*

Figure 2. From *castrum* to *colonia*: the evolution of Colchester *page 8*

Figure 3. Flavian *Verulamium page 11*

Figure 4. A: Silchester, urban centre of the Atrebates; B: the *vicus* at Water Newton *pages 13 and 14*

Figure 5. Part of south-west England and south-east Wales in the Roman period *page 15*

Figure 6. The *forum-basilica* complexes at A: London; and B: Silchester *page 17*

F⁀ure 7. The *forum-basilica* complexes at A: *Verulamium*; and B: Caerwent *page 18*

Figure 8. Restored view of the *forum-basilica* at Caerwent *page 18*

Figure 9. The *macella* at A: *Verulamium*; and B: Wroxeter *page 19*

Figure 10. The *mansio* at Silchester *page 20*

Figure 11. Restored view of the *mansio* at Silchester *page 21*

Figure 12. The *thermae* at A: Silchester; and B: Leicester *page 23*

Figure 13. Restored view of the *thermae* at Leicester *page 24*

Figure 14. The theatres at A: Canterbury; and B: *Verulamium page 25*

Figure 15. Early timber buildings at A: London; and B: *Verulamium page 30*

Figure 16. Restored view of an early timber building at *Verulamium page 30*

Figure 17. Typical house-plans at Silchester *page 31*

Figure 18. A: The 'compound-house' at Colliton Park, Dorchester; B: the 'courtyard-house' at Caerwent *page 33*

Figure 19. Sources of imported pottery to Sea Mills (*Abona*) *page 41*

Figure 20. Potteries and villas in the vicinity of Water Newton (*Durobrivae*) *page 45*

Figure 21. The Romano-Celtic temple at Caerwent *page 50*

Figure 22. A: The cemetery church at Butt Road, Colchester: plan and restored view; B: the decline of Roman Canterbury *page 53*

Plate 1. Inscription referring to the *Colonia Victricensis* at Colchester *page 9*

Plate 2. Inscription of the *respublica civitatis Silurum* (Caerwent) *page 12*

Plate 3. The *macellum* at Wroxeter *page 20*

Plate 4. The Old Work at Wroxeter, part of the Roman *thermae page 23*

Plate 5. The Jewry Wall at Leicester, part of the Roman *thermae page 24*

Plate 6. The theatre at *Verulamium page 26*

Plate 7. The Maumbury Rings at Dorchester: a Roman amphitheatre *page 27*

Plate 8. The Balkerne Gate, Colchester *page 28*

Plate 9. A strip-house being excavated in the *vicus* at Greta Bridge *page 31*

Plate 10. The compound-house at Colliton Park, Dorchester *page 34*

Plate 11. The courtyard-house at Pound Lane, Caerwent *page 34*

Plate 12. The Romano-Celtic temple at Caerwent *page 50*

Plate 13. Inscription recording a temple of Serapis at York *page 51*

Plate 14. The cemetery church at Butt Road, Colchester *page 54*

Plate 15. A tower on the south defences at Caerwent *page 68*

Plate 16. The blocked south gate of Caerwent *page 71*

Preface and acknowledgements

In preparing this third edition of *Towns in Roman Britain* I have remained conscious of my original aim: to provide a general introduction to the urbanisation of Roman Britain, useful to both the amateur and the student. Such was never a simple task, for there were some 110 urban communities in Britannia during the 366 years of direct Roman rule, each developing its own identity and character over this long period. Since the second edition of *Towns* appeared, however, the exercise has been made much more exacting – and equally more exciting – by the wealth of new data being produced through enhanced techniques and approaches to urban excavation. Hence this edition has been completely rewritten to make as much as possible of this new material available for the general reader. As it must remain a synthesis, however, rather than a detailed exposition, a comprehensive reading list is provided for those who want to know more about the subject.

A dilemma in a book like this is nomenclature. I have chosen to use modern place names throughout, except for *Verulamium*, now open fields near St Albans and always referred to by this name in the archaeological literature; the Roman names of most other places mentioned can, however, be found at the end of this book. Similarly, I have used the words 'city' or 'town' to define broadly the sites I discuss, not the very precise terms familiar to an administrator in the western Roman Empire. For him, the title of an urbanised settlement indicated the exact type and degree of autonomy of the place concerned, as a *colonia, municipium Latinum* or *Romanum, civitas, vicus* or *oppidum*. None of these titles has an exact parallel in modern English – especially as the term used to refer to a place today usually indicates its size and amenities rather than its position in the formal hierarchy of local and regional administration! Here, however, legalese must take precedence. Whatever the size of the urban settlement in Roman Britain (figure 1), I use the word 'city' for a chartered community, or urban settlement with self-governing rights (the *coloniae, municipia* and *civitates*); and 'town' for those urbanised communities which – no matter how large – lacked autonomy and were subordinate to a city (the *vici* and *oppida*).

The preparation of this third edition of *Towns* was at the suggestion of Sue Ross of Shire Publications Ltd. I thank her for the invitation to rewrite the book, and most especially for her patience, as I caught up with the archaeological developments of the past sixteen years. I would also like to thank Shannon Haley, Pınar Teker and Ayşe Tuğcu for helpful comments on an early draft of the text; Jean Greenhalgh, for her thorough dissection of a later version; İlkay Alpay, for ensuring the completion of the final version for publication; Jacques Morin, for help with computerese; Ben Claasz Coockson for the drawings; James Dyer, for modifying figure 7; Kevin Boddington, for digitising the illustrations; and J. Casey, C. Daniels, Cadbury Lamb, N. Hwmbo, the Musei e Gallerie Pontifice (Vatican), and the Yorkshire Museum (York), for assisting with the photographs. Dr Rosalind Niblett kindly read the proofs and provided information about recent findings at *Verulamium*. Finally I wish to acknowledge Dr Marie-Henriette Gates, my Head of Department, for her encouragement and support of my work.

JULIAN BENNETT
Arkeoloji ve Sanat Tarihi Bölümü,
Bilkent Üniversitesi, Ankara

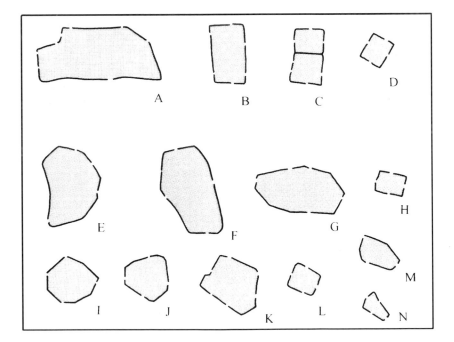

Figure 1. Comparative sizes of some walled towns in Roman Britain: A: London; B: Colchester; C: Lincoln; D: Gloucester; E: Wroxeter; F: Cirencester; G: *Verulamium*; H: Caistor-by-Norwich; I: Silchester; J: Chichester; K: Winchester; L: Caerwent; M: Water Newton; N: Rochester.

1
The urbanisation of Britain

The Roman invasion of Britain in AD 43 was initiated to secure the position of the new emperor Claudius. This single fact distinguishes Britannia from most other Roman provinces, annexed ostensibly for security reasons. Furthermore, for many years after, the garrison required to hold the territory probably cost Rome more than what the island returned in taxes, as anticipated by Strabo (*Geog.* 2.5.8). These two points are material to any review of the cities and towns of Britannia: Rome's guiding principle in ruling her dominion was to adapt indigenous forms of authority to her own requirements. The empire was sustained not by exploiting the provinces, but by fixing them in a specific alliance with Rome.

This approach was dictated by the desire to avoid a large and costly provincial bureaucracy. Rome preferred to adjust indigenous traditions of order to create a system in which provincial authority was delegated to a few suitable men as part of a formal hierarchy of public service. Rome's provincial governors, mostly senators, took office as a consequence of their social status, without any training, and with only a few friends as their executive staff. Their mandate was simple: to keep peace in their *provincia* (area of duty); and to ensure the relevant *tributa* (contributions) were collected for local expenses along with a share for Rome. After all, the aim of Roman imperialism was hegemony, not colonialism. While peace was maintained and taxes were paid, her foreign subjects were left alone: Rome assumed none of the burdens of economic development and the like carried by modern nation states.

This 'hands-off' system of control worked in the Mediterranean provinces with their long-established urban cultures. Once a garrison was installed for overall security, and a governor appointed for judicial procedure, a regular census was initiated to assess the *tributum solis*, on property, and the *tributum capitis*, or poll-tax. The existing local administration was responsible for collecting these and for local order, while a provincial council was formed from the élite of the indigenous communities to mediate between province and emperor. In Britannia, however, the procedure could not be imposed, for the island lacked a viable civil and political infrastructure. Instead, Rome was confronted with several tribal groupings rooted in a lineage and clan order, most people occupying small dispersed farming settlements, and ignorant of any monetary or taxation system.

The lack of any centralised political authority when Claudius invaded Britain is revealed by its many hillforts, evidence of a constant state of vendetta and feud. True, some early Roman writers described certain

British settlements as *oppida*, a term used for those large nucleated settlements of 'barbarian' Europe operating as regional centres of authority and trade. But while some British *oppida* were large dyked enclosures, most were small defended citadels, and none had the permanent populations or the commercial nature of their European analogues. In Britain, then, the term *oppidum* indicated a territorial centre, a focal point for tribal assemblies, whatever other social or economic role it played in local life.

Consequently, as in other parts of north-west Europe, the Romans had to invent a political and economic structure to manage the new province successfully. It was achieved by forming a series of self-governing civic regions, each a *respublica* or republic, a community with a

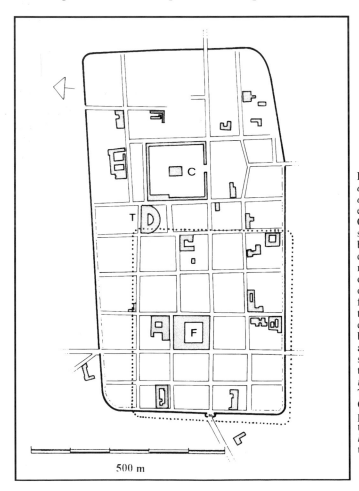

Figure 2. From *castrum* to *colonia*: the evolution of Colchester, showing known buildings. The dotted line marks the outline of the original fortress, and the eastern extension can be clearly seen, along with the streets forming the regular *insulae*. C: Temple of Claudius; F: probable site of the *forum-basilica*; T: theatre.

500 m

'democratic' constitution defining its relationship with Rome. It was an easy task in one respect, as all conquered territory was *ager publicus* (public land), for Rome to dispose of as required. Only those areas ruled by allied rulers, such as Prasutagus of the Iceni, Cogidubnus of the Regini, and Cartimandua of the Brigantes, were initially left intact, although these too came to Rome once their ruler died.

Foremost amongst the new communities in Britannia were the imperial *coloniae*, settlements of legionary veterans. Three were founded, each adapted from disused legionary fortresses, the first at Colchester in *c*.49 (figure 2), followed by Lincoln (*c*.83), and then Gloucester (*c*.90–6). A block of land (*territorium*) was defined for each, enough for every colonist to have about 50 *iugera* apiece (134 ha), along with a portion owned by the *colonia* for rental purposes, its *ager vectigalis*. The *territorium* was divided into a series of rectangular parcels for dispersal by lot, and many were later defined by hedges, ditches and trackways. These boundaries often survived into later times, and so, south of Gloucester, the framework of the original Roman allotment system can still be traced in the modern landscape.

As each *colonia* was a settlement of Roman citizens, it was legally part of Rome itself, and subject to a regular census to confirm their

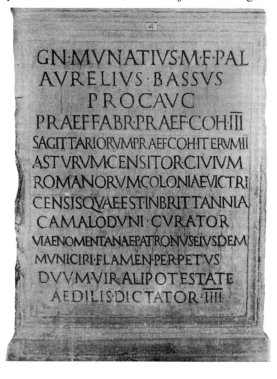

status (plate 1). A written code (*lex coloniae*) defined its required administration, with overall responsibility for government assumed by the *ordo*, a council of some hundred *decuriones* elected from among the colonists. They delegated matters to two pairs of annually

Plate 1. Inscription commemorating Gnaeus Munatius Aurelius Bassus, once in charge of the census of Roman citizens at *Colonia Victricensis, quae est in Britannia, Camaloduni* (*sic*): 'the Victory Colony, in Britain at Camulodunum' (Vatican Museum).

elected magistrates, who showed their gratitude for the honour by providing a public show or feast, or even a public building. The senior pair, the *duoviri iuridicundo*, took turns as chairman of the *ordo* and the law courts, while every fifth year they also became the census commissioners of the *colonia*. Their juniors, the *duoviri aediles*, assumed responsibility for maintaining public buildings and amenities, with the help of semi-permanent financial officers, the *quaestores*.

The imperial *coloniae* are often believed to have served two practical functions: as a reserve of trained men in the event of a revolt in a newly occupied province; and as models of Roman urban life towards which the natives could duly aspire. This is an oversimplification. While the *coloniae* may well have initially fulfilled a military role, their main purpose was to provide retired soldiers with land for their own use. And, as Rome desired peace above all to achieve her own needs, the small number of colonists involved were not expected to dominate their neighbours with a heavy hand. On the contrary, they had to establish a *modus vivendi* with local folk in order to exist in alien surroundings where they were greatly outnumbered, and only incidentally did they expose the native British to the refined technologies, amenities and luxuries characteristic of Roman urban communities.

The second class of urban community established in Rome's western provinces was the *municipium*. Generally formed from an existing native township, it was given a Romanised political and executive system and its own unique constitution, based on either Latin or Roman law. It seems that in a *municipium Latinum* the legal system combined Roman and local laws, the senior magistrates receiving Roman citizenship on election, while in a *municipium Romanum* only Roman law applied, and all who satisfied the property census might apply for Roman citizenship regardless of public service. Legal niceties apart, the motive for elevating aboriginal communities to municipal status was to encourage the adoption of Roman doctrine among a receptive local élite: it guaranteed the emergence of suitably 'Romanised' recruits for the future efficient government of the provinces.

The process worked in western regions that were familiar with Hellenising influences, such as Hispania. Britannia, however, lacked any tradition of urban settlement and civic organisation: therefore, an example was necessary as a pattern for future development. Hence the foundation of *Verulamium* in *c*.49 (figure 3), using land within the earlier *oppidum* of *Verlamion*, the social and religious focus of the Catuvellauni, where pre-conquest Italian wine amphorae indicate that a rich native tribal élite receptive to Roman ways already existed. We can infer that *Verulamium* was a *municipium Romanum*, and that it was given at least the minimum requirements of a classical city for its

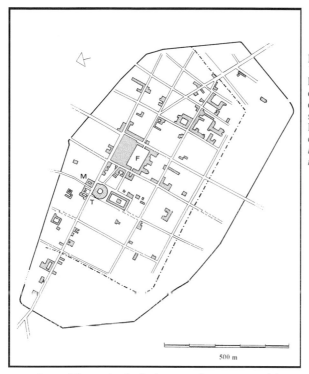

Figure 3. Flavian *Verulamium*, showing known buildings. The dotted line indicates the extent of the Flavian settlement, and the solid line that of the third-century town. F: *forum-basilica*; T: theatre; M: *macellum*.

populace. These included a regular street-grid, creating a series of land plots (*insulae*) of a consistent size, facilitating division of the area into zones for public, religious and private use; and material and practical help from the Roman administration for making the obligatory civic facilities at the settlement's centre.

Although *Verulamium* is the only certain *municipium* created in Britannia, Roman London also probably began as an imperially sponsored venture. When devastated by Boudicca in AD 61, it was a large and wealthy place, with a regular street-grid and a large population of Roman citizens – some traders, others of senior rank in the provincial administration. The lack of evidence for any intensive use of the site in pre-Roman times suggests that the Roman settlement was created to stimulate trade and immigration by Roman entrepreneurs to the most convenient inland port in the island. It was perhaps a *conventus civium Romanorum*, an officially encouraged but unchartered community of mainly Roman citizens, later promoted to a *municipium Romanum*.

Administrative necessity meant that other urban settlements appeared in Britannia, as new areas were given over to civilian control, and as allied rulers died and their territories were annexed. The existing tribal groupings provided the framework for the new system of administration, each becoming a *respublica* with a constitution based on local social,

Plate 2. Inscription commemorating Tiberius Claudius Paulinus, commander of the *Legio II Augusta*, erected by the *respublica civitatis Silurum*: 'the republic of the community of the Silures' (Caerwent).

political and legal traditions, and supervised by a political hierarchy formed from the native aristocracy (plate 2). As such, these communities were officially designated *civitates perigrinorum*, 'communities of aliens', and Rome took the minimum amount of responsibility for their development. All that was required was to select a suitable location for the necessary *civitas* centre, the urban focus required for the administration of the *civitas* by means of its essential *ordo* and *decuriones*, with an appropriate *territorium* for the use of its population. Generally, the place picked for the purpose was close to the tribe's pre-Roman social, religious or political centre, and often – as at Cirencester – on land originally appropriated as an army base to supervise this in the conquest period. Accordingly, while these settlements took a local indigenous toponym, the tribal name was added to show its status as the administrative centre of the *civitas*: hence *Venta Silurum*, 'Market of the Silures' (Caerwent), and *Ratae Corieltavorum*, 'Fortification of the Corieltavi' (Leicester).

We know almost nothing about the procedure involved in establishing the *civitas* centres. As early farms or villas are generally lacking within 15 km of them, we can assume their *territoria* covered substantial areas and were divided into regular plots for future distribution, some presumably assigned to the local tribal élite according to their wealth and status, the rest probably becoming the property of the *civitas*, as *ager vectigalis*. Otherwise, Rome's active involvement in forming the urban centres of the *civitates* seems restricted to establishing a basic street-grid, as at Silchester, centre for the Atrebates (figure 4A). It was left to each *civitas* to supply the required urban facilities from its own resources, although Claudius granted cash to some tribal élites for this purpose, and at least one governor, Agricola, provided logistical help. Even so, as Tacitus makes clear, the gullible *nouveau riche* of south Britain, eager for new fashions, soon adopted the new forms of public

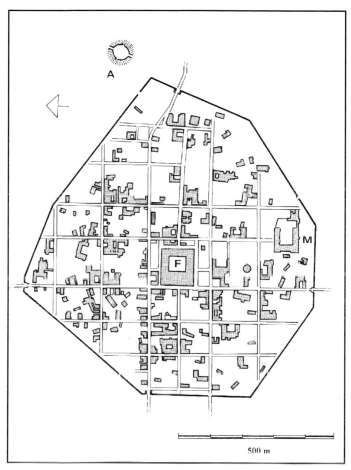

Figure 4A.
Silchester, the
urban centre of
the Atrebates,
showing the
known buildings.
F: *forum-
basilica*; A:
amphitheatre; M:
mansio.

500 m

architecture, as well as the clothing and social pleasures of the
conquerors: 'They spoke of such novelties as "civilisation", when this
was really only a feature of their slavery' (Tacitus *Agr.* 21). Indeed,
Rome's main achievement in Britain was in persuading the most
backward of its dependencies to accept urbanisation and classical culture.

The other urbanised settlements of Britannia were the *vici*, easily
identified by their lack of regular planning and public administrative
buildings. The term *vicus* defined a settlement with no autonomy in
Roman law and subject to a chartered community or military base,
whatever its own size. Most British *vici* fall into the military category,
the forts and fortresses being homes of bachelor soldiers with money to
burn, luring many civilians willing to assist them. These initially
transitory settlements, providing the trading and leisure facilities required

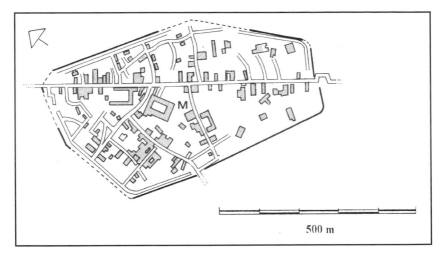

500 m

Figure 4B. The *vicus* at Water Newton, from aerial photographs showing known streets and buildings and the *mansio* (M): note the irregular street-plan of this *vicus*, compared with the regular *insulae* at Colchester, *Verulamium* and Silchester.

by the soldiers, became durable townships when the unit they served ceased operating as a mobile force and became a fixed garrison. As such, the military *vici* were supervised by the local unit commander and might even assume responsibility for working the adjacent land and feeding the garrison. Being thriving entities, they also attracted retired veterans, for many were loath to leave familiar environs, their concubine and their family after twenty-five years of service. Thus, some military *vici*, like Housesteads, became larger than the adjacent fort and significantly expanded in the third century, once soldiers could legally marry.

Many of the civilian *vici* in Britannia began as military *vici* in the conquest period, but they later prospered because the number of chartered communities in the province was small compared with the extensive territories they served. This abetted the growth of ancillary commercial and industrial centres at distances more appropriate for regional commerce: hence most civilian *vici* are situated about 15–30 km from one another along the main roads, suitable for serving 'territories' with up to a day's return journey from outlying farms (figure 5). Some became quite wealthy and large, such as Water Newton, the focus of a major pottery industry in the late third and early fourth centuries (figure 4B), but most, like Sea Mills, were nothing more than large villages, providing local market facilities.

Political, economic and social developments changed the formal status of certain Roman-British cities and towns. *Vici* with resident Roman

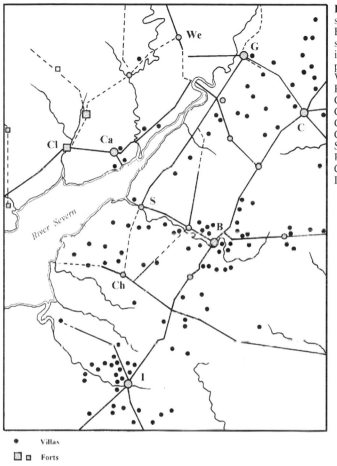

Figure 5. Part of south-west England and south-east Wales in the Roman period. We: Weston under Penyard; Cl: Caerleon fortress; Ca: Caerwent; G: Gloucester; C: Cirencester; S: Sea Mills; B: Bath; Ch: Charterhouse; I: Ilchester.

●   Villas

▢ ◻   Forts

◯ ⊙   Towns

citizens, for example, might be permitted to establish a semi-autonomous local government on the Roman model, with an elected *ordo* and *aediles*. Inscriptions indicate this happened at the military *vicus* at Old Carlisle and the civilian *vicus* at Brough-on-Humber. More significant changes came with periodic reorganisations of the provincial administration. The *vicus* opposite the legionary fortress at York, for one, was probably given municipal status during Hadrian's visit to Britannia in 122, and it was perhaps also then that some lesser tribal groups subsumed into larger *civitates* gained autonomy. The *civitas* of the Brigantes, for instance, centred on Aldborough, was divided to form the additional *respublicae* of the Carvetti, based on Carlisle, the Corionototae, with its centre at Corbridge, and the Parisii, focused on Brough-on-Humber. Likewise the Dematae, affiliated with the Dobunni, were eventually given autonomy and a new urban centre next to the military *vicus* at Carmarthen, while the *civitas Durotrages*, based on Dorchester, was also subdivided, the area around Ilchester becoming an independent *civitas perigrinorum*.

The impetus for these changes was probably increased imperial control over the *civitates*. There was an economic boom throughout the Roman Empire in the second century, as shown by the many large public buildings of this period found in every province. However, in a system where regional government was controlled by locally elected amateurs, civic funds were often mismanaged or used on grandiose public amenities which were badly designed or underfinanced. Trajan's momentous decision in 111 to make Pliny the Younger *curator* (auditor) of finances in Bithynia signalled imperial anxiety about how provincial moneys were being spent. Hadrian's subdivision of the larger British *civitates* into smaller units affirmed the need for greater control over local affairs, with imperial *curatores* to supervise municipal matters and finances.

In practice, the use of *curatores* to manage civic affairs more efficiently seems to have had a detrimental effect, for in Britannia, as elsewhere, the late second century was marked by a decline in public investment in urban facilities. Quite why this was so is not fully understood, but part of the problem was probably the authority of the *curatores* over civic expenditure. It deterred local aristocracies from standing for public office as they could no longer choose how to use their own money for their community. As their donations withered, the *curatores* imposed higher taxes on them and their communities to maintain existing facilities and amenities, increasing disaffection and eliminating the benefits of local public office. As even fewer of the local élite voluntarily assumed the burdens of civic office, civic building in the urban communities of Britannia effectively came to a halt by *c*.200.

2
Public buildings and amenities

The only contemporary source suggesting Rome deliberately urbanised any of its provinces is in the biography of Agricola, governor of Britannia in 77–83. According to Tacitus, its author, the absence of civic organisation in Britain before the Roman invasion meant that the people were prone to 'anarchy'. Consequently, Agricola provided suitable communal amenities and facilities, such as temples and public squares, to promote amity, using his own resources and unspecified 'official assistance' for the purpose (Tacitus *Agr.* 21). For Tacitus, then, the existence of the appropriate public infrastructure was the defining characteristic of a Roman city, a view confirmed by a later writer who questioned the official status of *Phokis* in Greece as a 'city', as it lacked civic offices, leisure facilities, a market area and a public water supply (Pausanias 10.3.4).

These sources indicate that the status of any community in the Roman period was expressed through its civic architecture and infrastructure. Yet while the state might provide some logistical assistance for the purpose, the main costs were borne by the community alone and its more affluent citizens. This meant that in Britannia – and elsewhere – the newly founded communities were slow to develop an urban character, a generation or more passing before the first civic architecture appeared

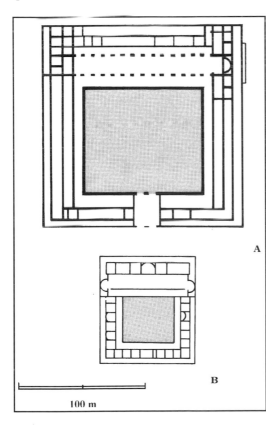

Figure 6. The *forum-basilica* complexes at London (A) and Silchester (B).

A

B

100 m

18

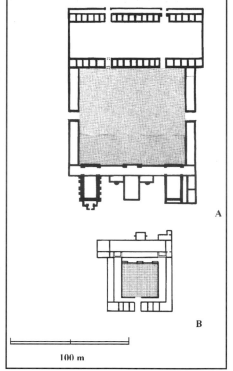

Figure 7. The *forum-basilica* complexes at *Verulamium* (A) (James Dyer, after Niblett) and Caerwent (B). The details of the *Verulamium* basilica are largely conjectural.

A

B

100 m

at most *civitas* centres. Even so, it seems that the main priority for the new cities was to construct the facilities required for their administration. For this reason, the first structure built in most Roman-British cities was the *forum-basilica* complex, usually at the centre of the urban area.

The *basilica* was the seat of government and justice for the community (figures 6–8). It was a large aisled hall, equal in size to the naves of many medieval cathedrals, with a raised area at one end for the magistrates to judge law cases and oversee council meetings, and offices along one side for the *duoviri* and their clerks. The *forum*, on the other hand, was both the formal meeting place of a city and its business centre, a place where official announcements were made, elections were held, and money-lenders and traders negotiated matters. The civic role explains the plan and location of the *forum*, an enclosed square to one side of the *basilica*; its economic

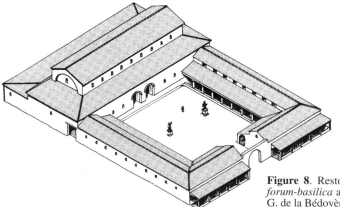

Figure 8. Restored view of the *forum-basilica* at Caerwent (after G. de la Bédoyère).

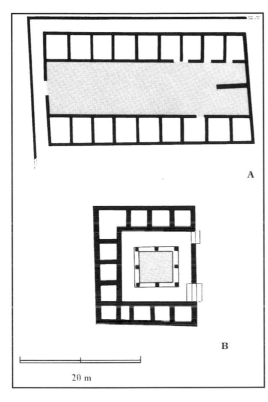

Figure 9. The *macella* at *Verulamium* (A) and Wroxeter (B: see also plate 3).

function arose from its pivotal position in public life and activity, making it the logical place for business dealings. Consequently, the *forum* had colonnaded ranges on its other three sides, providing shelter during inclement weather, with rooms behind for municipal and commercial purposes.

The compact enclosed plan of the *forum-basilica* complexes in almost all the British cities is very distinct in the Roman world. A few examples in Italy excepted, it finds parallels in the *principia* (headquarters building) of Roman forts and fortresses, and the *fora-basilicae* of imperial *coloniae*, themselves often adapted from an earlier legionary *principia*. Elsewhere in the western Roman Empire a very different plan was usual, the *forum* being surrounded by porticoes rather than colonnaded ranges, with a temple central to one side of the square, flanked or faced by offices for the *ordo* and the magistrates. In Britannia, however, this arrangement is seen only at *Verulamium* (figure 7A), and the similarity of the remainder to the military *principia* could well be explained by military involvement in their design and construction – perhaps the 'official assistance' referred to by Tacitus in his eulogy of Agricola.

In addition to a *forum-basilica*, some cities in Britannia also had a *macellum* or covered market, used solely for retail trade, and underscoring how the *pax Romana*, the Roman Peace, inspired surplus production and greater trading activity. The *macellum* at Leicester consisted of an aisled hall and courtyard, with at least one lateral colonnaded wing. Those at *Verulamium* and Wroxeter (figure 9) were smaller, the first with two rows of rooms facing each other across an open area, the second (plate 3) being a colonnaded courtyard, with three ranges of rooms as well as a latrine in one angle. While none of them

Plate 3. The *macellum* at Wroxeter (see also figure 9B).

has produced unequivocal proof of commercial activity, their utilitarian plans and proximity to their respective *fora* tend to undermine other suggestions regarding their purpose.

Of less significance to everyday matters in any city or town, but indicating its status in the Roman administrative scheme, was the *mansio*, or hostel. The Roman Empire was managed through rapid communications effected by the *cursus publicus*, the imperial messenger service. *Mansiones* were provided at regular intervals on all primary routes to provide lodgings and spare mounts for these official travellers, and also for those on private business, and such facilities have been identified at Wall, Caerwent and Silchester. They were two-storeyed buildings with rooms and stabling arranged around a courtyard, somewhat like a late-medieval coaching inn, but often with a *balneum*, or bath-suite, as well (figures 10–11). Official itineraries, like the *Tabula Peutingeriana*, gave travellers

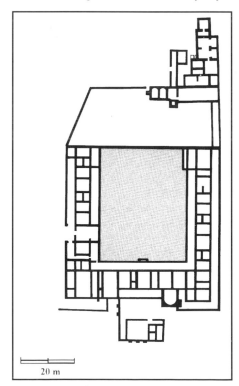

20 m

Figure 10. The *mansio* at Silchester.

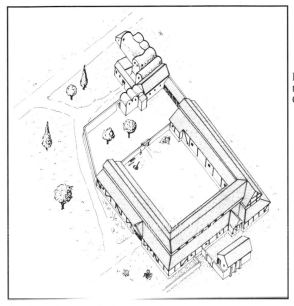

Figure 11. Restored view of the *mansio* at Silchester (after G. de la Bédoyère).

the locations and distances between the *mansiones*, and symbols indicated the different amenities available at each.

It was the publicly sponsored hydraulic infrastructure of Roman cities which above all distinguished them from other urban settlements of the past. Water is heavy, and the hauling and carrying of the required daily quantity from wells or streams was a thankless yet necessary task. The provision of a public water supply and fountains was accordingly a matter of great communal benefit, involving a high degree of expertise to provide water at the required volume and appropriate velocity. As such, the building of an aqueduct was a matter of proper civic pride, and subconsciously reinforced a sense of stability and order among the population, confirming the benefits of organised local government under the watchful eye of the provincial governor.

We might assume that all Roman-British cities and many towns had an aqueduct, even if it were a sub-surface conduit rather than one of the arcaded systems familiar elsewhere in the Roman Empire. It is true that the Lincoln aqueduct used an arched bridge to cross a stream, and that the Leicester example was partly embanked: but these are exceptions. Indeed, a preference for conduits shows good economic sense by the engineers, as elevated channels were costly to build and maintain and were provided only when essential. This did not absolve the builders from making accurate hydraulic calculations and precise ground surveys: the 18 km long conduit that supplied Dorchester, for example, has an average drop of 38 cm per km, and its cross-section of 60 by 90 cm allowed a constant flow of about 59 million litres per day.

All aqueducts delivered their water to a filtering and distribution cistern (*castellum divisiorium*), although none in Britannia compares to the *nymphaea*, the elaborate versions of these usual in the eastern provinces. It was then fed to public fountains and, occasionally, to private houses, usually in wooden pipes coupled with iron collars. How many fountains may have existed in any one city is uncertain, although at *Pompeii* no house was more than 80 metres from one. That apart, a basic problem with a gravity-fed aqueduct system is that the source cannot be turned off, and so ample drainage is essential; if not provided, the streets would be awash with the surplus overflow from the fountains, the real reason why substantial drains existed in many Roman-British cities.

Drains of this type, therefore, were never specifically planned as sewers, although they were often used in this way for the communal latrines occasionally provided in public buildings. These took the form of wooden or stone seats in line over a deep sewer, 'flushed' by a constant flow of water, and with an open gutter in front of the seats for cleaning the sponges used as toilet paper. Such facilities were rare; private toilets were more usual, although of the most basic kind. In these, the solid waste ('night soil') amassed in a box or pit beneath the seat, to be recycled as highly valued manure. Urine, on the other hand, was collected in jars, also for recycling, as an essential agent in the tanning and fulling processes: indeed, the parsimonious emperor Vespasian taxed fullers for urine collected from the jars they provided as public urinals!

An adequate water supply was more especially needed to supply a city's *thermae*, its bath-house. First on the list of public amenities in the Roman world, these were ancestral to the modern Turkish bath, relying on inducing perspiration by a series of rooms heated to increasing temperatures. The system depended on the hypocaust, an underfloor heating method using hot air from external stokeholes, and circulated through channels beneath an internal floor raised on brick or stone pillars (plate 4) before passing up the inner surface of the walls via hollow tiles. The combination of cavity floors and walls ensured that the minimum of heat was lost, and little attention was required for the furnaces once they were fired.

Most British *thermae*, like that at Silchester (figure 12A), had the single axial plan of bath-houses used by a small clientele. A few, however, as at Leicester (figures 12B and 13, and plate 5), had a double-circulation system, with parallel sets of heated rooms, a plan usual when there was a much greater demand. Whatever the plan, the sequence of bathing was the same. After disrobing in the *apodyterium*, the bather passed through the *frigidarium* (cold room) to the *tepidarium* (warm room), pausing to acclimatise to the increased temperature. Then he entered the intensely hot and humid *caldarium*, to promote the heavy

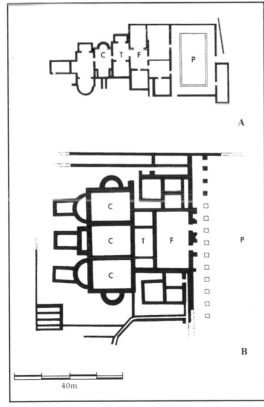

Plate 4. The Old Work at Wroxeter, part of the Roman *thermae:* the wall originally divided the *palaestra* from the *tepidarium* with its hypocaust, visible in the foreground. (Charles Daniels)

A

B

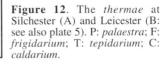

40m

Figure 12. The *thermae* at Silchester (A) and Leicester (B: see also plate 5). P: *palaestra*; F: *frigidarium*; T: *tepidarium*; C: *caldarium*.

24

Figure 13.
Restored view of
the *thermae* at
Leicester (after
D. S. Neal).

sweating which was the purpose of the process, although some favoured the dry heat of the *laconium* instead. After a suitable period, the bather was scoured with a *strigil* and sponge to remove dead skin and dirt, before returning to the *tepidarium* for a massage with olive oil, and thence to the *frigidarium* to dive into the cold water pool (*natatio*), to close the skin pores and prevent a chill.

Plate 5. The Jewry Wall at Leicester, part of the Roman *thermae* (see also figure 12B): the wall once divided the *palaestra*, beneath the church on the right, from the *frigidarium* and *apodyteria* in the foreground.

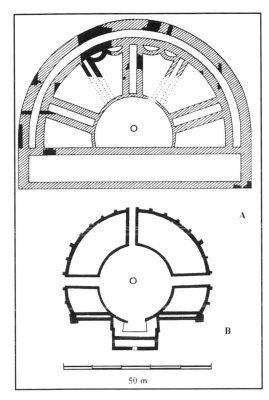

Figure 14. The theatres at Canterbury (A) and *Verulamium* (B: see also plate 6).

Communal bathing was an established part of the Roman social system, the *thermae* being where all met on equal terms for their ablutions and all the other pleasantries of a superior community centre. As such, they often had a *palaestra*, an exercise area for those who wanted to practise sports or keep fit. Others might indulge in less strenuous activities, gossip and gambling being popular. However, while other cities in the Roman Empire often had two or more *thermae*, the British were apparently loath to adopt the concept of public bathing: London apart, it seems that no city in Britannia had more than one public bath-house, while those found in the civilian *vici* are always part of a *mansio*. Even so, when viewing the paltry remains of those that survive today, one should visualise them as they once were, places where there was

> All sorts of noise, enough to make you hate your ears! Toughs exercise, throwing their hands about with weights, grunting each time they expel treasured breath … [And] the noise of some quarrelsome fellow, or a thief caught in the act, or the man who loves the sound of his own voice in the bath – not to mention those who belly-flop with a tremendous splash. Also the strident cry of the depilator, incessantly advertising his presence, only quiet when – plucking someone's armpits – his client cries out for him; and the shouts of the pastry cook, the sausage seller, the confectioner, and the hawkers of refreshments …
>
> (Seneca *Ep. Mor.* 61.1–2).

Other than the *thermae*, the principal public amenities found in a Roman provincial city were structures for *spectaculae* – entertainment: theatres, mainly for comedy and pantomimes; amphitheatres, for gladiatorial fights – men against men, and men against beasts – as well as boxing and wrestling bouts; and stadia, for equestrian and track

Plate 6. The theatre at *Verulamium* (see also figure 14B): the almost circular orchestra can be clearly seen, with two of the opposing side entrances; the stage building is on the left, and the wooden seats rose on tiers on the earthen banks. (Cadbury Lamb, by courtesy of Gorhambury Estates Company)

events. Although theatres might be expected at each city, only four are known, at *Verulamium*, Colchester, Canterbury and – from an inscription – at Brough-on-Humber. Those at Colchester and Canterbury (figure 14A) have the typical plan and structural framework of a Roman theatre, tiers of seats raised on radial foundation walls, and a large stage building closing a D-shaped orchestra. That at *Verulamium*, on the other hand (figure 14B and plate 6), was closer in form to a Hellenistic theatre, with seats on a crescent-shaped earthen bank, and an almost circular orchestra and small stage building. The plan is entirely suitable for Hellenic drama alone, the actors and chorus performing in the orchestra rather than on the stage. It suggests an inherent conservatism among the early inhabitants of *Verulamium*, evidently maintained for generations: when the theatre was remodelled in the third century, the same basic plan was kept, with only minor changes to the overall form.

Examples of civic amphitheatres are more numerous and are known at London, Caistor-by-Norwich, Carmarthen, Dorchester (plate 7), Silchester, Chichester and Cirencester, all with the usual elliptical form with opposed entrances, and tiers of seats rising on timber- or stone-revetted banks. Other evidence for gladiators in Britannia includes a graffito at Leicester and a helmet found near Colchester. On the other hand, the complementary distribution of those British cities with theatres and those with amphitheatres suggests that – as in other provinces – the theatres might be modified with raised walls around the orchestra for

Plate 7. The Maumbury Rings at Dorchester, a Roman amphitheatre, converted from an earlier Neolithic henge monument, and used in the seventeenth century in the Civil War as an artillery position. The arena is the flat area in the middle, and the wooden seats rose in tiers above the earth banks.

gladiatorial shows. As for stadia, however, there is no clear evidence from any city or town in Britannia, suggesting a lack of interest in equestrian or track events, although these could have taken place in a suitably flat area without built structure. That said, permanent circuses intended specifically for chariot-races were often constructed where an emperor spent any length of time, and so examples may well yet be discovered at both York and London.

No self-respecting Roman community lacked the last category of civic architecture, honorific monuments. Neither facility nor amenity, these were simply a visible record of some event or service involving the community, and consequently they were usually erected in or near the *forum*, the place where public and civic unity was asserted. Most took the form of an inscribed base commemorating a benefaction by a local official, as with the pedestal at Caerwent honouring Tiberius Claudius Paulinus, commander of the *Legio II Augusta* at nearby Caerleon (plate 2). Those honouring an emperor, on the other hand, often carried a stone or bronze statue. Thus the *colonia* at Colchester was originally graced with a life-size statue in bronze of Claudius, and an over-life-size statue of Hadrian once stood in some public place in London, while the *fora* at Lincoln and Gloucester contained life-size equestrian statues of unidentified emperors.

Equally impressive were the arches (*fornices*), the vaulted passageways dedicated to a specific emperor, set up to commemorate a military

Plate 8. The Balkerne Gate, all that survives of Claudius's victory arch at Colchester.

victory or a personal visit, or just to express the loyalty of the community to its ruler. And yet, despite the many campaigns and imperial visits to Britannia, only one imperial *fornix* is known in a civil context, that originally dedicated to Claudius and his British victory, which later became the core of Colchester's Balkerne Gate (plate 8). It was also common for cities and even individual citizens to erect smaller archways for some reason. Such were the arch for the god Viridius at Ancaster, built by a local man, Trenico; the third-century arch for the Olympian gods at London; and the arch honouring Jupiter Dolichenus, the emperors and the *genii loci* – the 'spirits of the place' – built at York by Viducius Placidus ('a Gaul, merchant with Britannia').

3
Housing and households

The street-grid and *insulae* (land plots) common to the chartered cities of Britannia (for example, figures 3–4) allowed the allotment of appropriate areas for public and private use, separate plots in the residential zones being assigned for individual development. How these were distributed is unclear, except in the case of the *coloniae*, where a veteran received his portion by imperial gift, the size being determined by rank and service record. At Lincoln and Gloucester the evidence suggests a group of men received an existing military barrack block within the defunct fortress as their minimum urban grant, for there was little immediate change to the internal arrangements of these places, the existing street-grid and many buildings being retained almost unaltered at both. At Colchester, on the other hand, major alterations were made to the site when it became a *colonia*. While the west part of the fortress layout was retained, along with its existing buildings, the east part was redesigned with new streets on a slightly different alignment to include extra land for development as a residential, religious and ceremonial focus (figure 2). As a result, slightly larger *insulae* are found in this more prestigious area of the colony and, as more luxurious houses were built here in later years, they may well have been allotted to veterans of senior rank.

How the private *insulae* in the other urban centres of Britannia were originally allocated is uncertain. As *ager publicus*, they were probably granted or sold to members of the local aristocracy, who apportioned and then leased, assigned or sold separate plots to their clients, subordinates and others. This is suggested by a comparison of the size and arrangements of the *insulae* in the *coloniae* with those in the lesser cities. In the *coloniae* many individual plots remained undivided for decades (Colchester apart, due to the Boudiccan Revolt), implying they were inherited complete. In London, *Verulamium* and the *civitas* centres, on the other hand, the number, orientation and size of individual land plots within the *insulae* often varied greatly over time, hinting at frequent changes in ownership. Moreover, while the *insulae* in the *coloniae* were often used exclusively for residential purposes, those in the lesser cities frequently contained buildings that combined a residence with a manufacturing centre and shop, again suggesting they were divided into leased properties. Indeed, the purchase and development of such allotments most probably occasioned loans of the type the philosopher Seneca made to certain British nobles: in his case, these totalled 10 million *drachma* (Dio *Rom. Hist.* 62.2), a quantity of silver equivalent

30

Figure 15. Early timber buildings at London (A) and *Verulamium* (B).

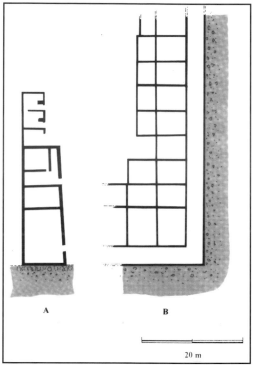

to about £5,600,000 in 2001.

Within the *coloniae* the evidence indicates that the first inhabitants either modified the standing military timber buildings for their own requirements or constructed new ones on a similar pattern. The evidence for the other cities in the early decades of Roman rule in Britain is much more limited. At *Verulamium* one *insula* seems to have been developed as a single block, but the basic building unit was usually the strip-house, a long narrow structure with one short end facing the main street, and often used as a shop or business premises, with rooms behind for production, storage and residential purposes (figures 15, 16 and 17A, and plate 9). The choice of plan and orientation was probably inspired by anticipated economic gain, as land

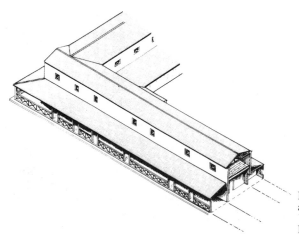

Figure 16. Restored view of an early timber building at *Verulamium* (after G. de la Bédoyère).

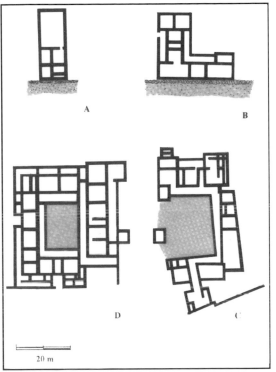

Figure 17. Typical house-plans at Silchester.

was usually at a premium in cities, especially in business and commercial areas. By this method, a landowner could fit several buildings into an *insula* and anticipate a greater rental return. However, one thing which sets the urban communities of Britannia apart from those elsewhere in the Roman Empire is the existence of large areas of open space within them. Caerwent excepted, it seems that none of the Roman-British cities was ever densely occupied (for example, Silchester, figure 4A). Thus, while economic motives might have prompted the strip house plan in the first place, it is likely that the owners never realised the return on capital they envisaged.

The earliest private urban buildings in Britannia were invariably built

Plate 9. A strip-house being excavated in the *vicus* at Greta Bridge. (J. Casey)

of wood. The choice of timber over brick or stone for construction was influenced by economic factors and local tradition. Stands of mature timber were available in most regions of Britannia, but outcrops of suitable building stone were less common, and harder to work and transport, while fired brick was used principally as a facing medium rather than a structural component. In areas where there was suitable building stone, it was often used for the base-walls of timber-framed structures, but daub or mud-brick remained the preferred walling medium: it was not only easier to fabricate than shaping stone blocks, or moulding and firing bricks, but it also had greater insulation properties, reflecting the warmth of long hot summer days to provide a cool interior, and retaining internal heat in the winter.

Visualising the appearance of the strip-houses is limited by the type of evidence available, normally just the foundation trenches used for the horizontal base-plates. Nonetheless, the use of simple and humble materials did not necessarily mean they were modest in structural terms. In London, for example, surviving timber base-plates and uprights reveal that complex carpentry skills were common and would have been adequate for building structures of two or more storeys. Whether London or any other Roman-British city was provided with multi-storey tenements is uncertain, although the narrow rooms in some strip-house buildings at *Verulamium* and elsewhere may well be stairwells to an upper storey (figures 15B and 16). As Roman law gave property rights from the ground to the sky, it might have seemed obvious to build multi-storey premises as investment holdings, anticipating a housing demand in city centres. Still, while the technical ability certainly existed, and some multi-storey private buildings are likely to have been constructed, they were probably uncommon. Such is implied by the large open spaces to be found in most cities and towns as well as the relative rarity of urban cellars: both factors point to the lack of any pressure to maximise the available land within a community and imply that multi-storey urban buildings were the exception rather than the rule.

The basic strip-house plan suited almost indefinite extension. Indeed, as populations became more prosperous and families grew larger, this is apparently what happened in many Roman-British cities and towns. Where several such properties existed in one *insula*, however, enlargement was usually only possible by adding extra rooms at the rear of the property, a covered passageway sometimes being provided along one side of the building for shelter when passing between the front and the rear additions (for example, figure 15A). More practical, if possible, was to extend the building sideways, usually by building new rooms or even complete wings at right-angles to the original structure,

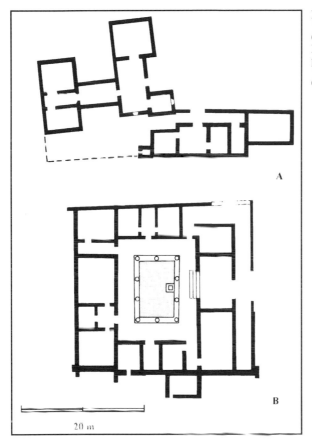

Figure 18. (A) The 'compound-house' at Colliton Park, Dorchester (see also plate 10). (B) The 'courtyard-house' at Caerwent.

with connecting corridors or porticoes (figure 17B). It had the effect of creating a semi-enclosed compound, which could now became the focus of the layout, especially if it was walled off and provided with a gateway (figures 17C and 18A; plates 10 and 11). Then, if further rooms were needed, a fourth wing could be added, eventually forming the fully enclosed compound-house seen in many Roman-British cities and towns (figure 17D).

The evolutionary process envisaged here may well have been typical in many urban settlements in Britannia. Clear evidence is scarce, not least because much of the 'evidence' for urban housing in Britannia has to be recycled from reports of explorers' relatively crude work of the nineteenth and early twentieth centuries, or from analyses of aerial photographs. On the other hand, a number of excavations since 1945

Plate 10. The compound-house at Colliton Park, Dorchester (see also figure 18A): the modern wooden building shelters a mosaic floor.

Plate 11. The compound-house at Pound Lane, Caerwent: traces of an earlier strip-house are visible beneath the later walls.

confirm that this evolutionary process was at least not uncommon. Even so, while the model need not have a strict chronological validity, the ubiquity of the process shows that free space into which to expand could be found next to many buildings in most Roman-British settlements, confirming that urban property was not in great demand in the province.

The sprawling compound-houses found in urban Britannia are quite distinct from the courtyard-houses of the contemporary Mediterranean world. These were designed and built as a single unit, the colonnaded courtyard being the focus of the whole layout and surrounded by rooms on all four sides. Such houses were built for an elevated social class, and we might speculate that the residences of the imperial governors and other officials which once existed at London and York were of this type. However, this inward-looking plan, eminently appropriate to the Mediterranean climate for which it was designed, giving shelter and shade from the extreme summer heat, was hardly necessary in the wetter and cooler climate of Britannia. Indeed, apart from at military bases, where it was the usual form of housing for senior officers, only four are known, two at Colchester, and single examples at Gloucester and Caerwent. Of these, the Colchester structures seem derived from the peristyle house familiar in the Hellenic world, the courtyard being essentially an open garden space for relaxation and leisure. Those at Gloucester and Caerwent (figure 18B), however, are closer to an Italic model, the atrium house, in which the courtyard is a more confined area. While none of these buildings is exactly like its Mediterranean archetype, they are still best explained as being designed for men of high social status familiar with accommodation of this type, especially as the Caerwent example was linked to the public water supply. As Colchester and Gloucester began as *coloniae*, and Caerwent is close to the legionary fortress at Caerleon, we might assume the householders were retired senior legionary officers of non-British origin. In this case the 'Italic' houses at Gloucester and Caerwent, and the 'Hellenic' example at Colchester, could well indicate the origins of these men.

The individual ground plans of urban residences in Britannia can suggest their external appearance, but archaeology adds details which can only be guessed at from plans alone. For example, the outer walls of some buildings at Caerwent were plastered, with incised and painted lines used to look like dressed ashlar rather than the rough-coursed masonry actually employed. Such finishes were probably common for most buildings, as an external rendering is essential to prevent water penetration of the walls, whether of stone, timber or mud-brick. As for the number and size of any window openings, however, we have almost no evidence, although most were probably shuttered, as finds of window-glass are uncommon in Britannia. Likewise, the rarity of tiles in urban contexts suggests that most roofs would have been thatched, although shingles cannot be excluded.

Much more is known of the interiors of town houses in Britannia, although it needs stressing that the information we have comes mainly from the houses of the prosperous, rather than from a broad cross-section of society. In the early years of Roman rule, the ground floors of almost all houses were of clay or beaten earth, no matter what the social class of the occupant was, although at a few sites in London planked floors supported on timber joists were provided. Flagged floors were rare except in those areas where suitable stone was available, and even then they were normally provided only in rooms used for commercial purposes. In later times, however, more prosperous citizens often had hypocausted floors installed in some rooms, usually with mosaic pavements over them. The walls of such rooms were often decorated with polychrome frescoes, sometimes of architectural and landscape scenes, more often with geometric patterns using large coloured panels – generally red, blue or green – divided by borders of white, to imitate marble veneer. A few houses even had painted ceilings, as has been shown from remains excavated at *Verulamium* and at Leicester.

Very little is known about how individual rooms might have been used in everyday private life. In the larger and more elaborate residences of the rich and powerful, we might assume that the more lavishly decorated rooms were for semi-public purposes. However, it is often impossible to identify the use of any single room or groups of rooms in such buildings, with the rare exception of private bath-suites. Possible functions can sometimes be inferred from individual details and the overall plan of the building, suggesting which rooms were *cubicula* (bedrooms), which were kitchens, and which were *triclinia* (dining suites), but there is no certainty in the matter. In fact, in large and small urban houses alike, many of the rooms probably served several functions and purposes at different times in the day. In bigger homes kitchens might become bedrooms overnight for servants or slaves, and the smaller rooms may have been bed-sitting rooms. Moreover, the function of a room often changed with time: what had been a study could have become a child's room – or might even have been rented to someone outside the family for financial reasons.

Likewise, we cannot say very much about how the individual rooms were furnished. The evidence is meagre and one-sided, with only a handful of material remains – and these mainly from the more opulent houses. From sculptural evidence we learn that the usual range of contemporary internal furnishings was available in Britannia, such as wing-backed chairs, stools, and couches of a chaise-longue type used as both day- and night-beds. They were made mainly of wood, sometimes of basketry, with leather or textile covers over a woollen stuffing. These materials rarely survive in the archaeological record, and so the evidence for their existence is generally limited to their metal fittings – the curved ends of armrests and couches, and the struts of folding 'camp-stools'. Other furniture included tripod tables, often with stone tops, and sometimes with metal or shale legs, while cupboards, chests and jewellery boxes are suggested by bronze and iron lock-plates, brackets and other fittings. A range of smaller furnishings and fittings, such as baskets, must also have been usual in domestic settings but, aside from vessels connected with cooking and eating, the most common finds are normally the small oil-lamps used to provide illumination at night.

The wealthy, who could afford to live in such luxury, were a minority in the towns and cities of Britannia. Most people lived in relative squalor, many sharing a single room with rushes over clay or earth floors. In such dwellings furniture was rare and, from skeletons of Roman date examined at sites in Italy, it is clear that the majority in any urban population never had the luxury of a proper chair but instead squatted on their haunches or on low stools. Beds likewise were simple, little more than a straw- or cloth-filled palliasse with a textile covering, as with the example found at Colchester, a carbonised relic of the Boudiccan Revolt. Lighting, if available, was by rush-torch.

4
Wealth, commerce and industry

The economy of pre-Roman Britain was like that of any non-industrialised society. Most of the population were employed in agriculture, and a relatively small élite owned the bulk of the land, the principal measure and source of wealth. In such systems, farming methods are usually underdeveloped, geared towards producing a sufficiency rather than a surplus, and the very few manufacturing industries which do exist are generally small-scale, making only those goods in local demand.

All this changed with the arrival of the Romans. While we do not know how the Roman authorities redistributed the land in the *civitates*, it stimulated an exponential growth in agricultural production and thus the economy. This is shown archaeologically by an increase in the number of farms between the late first and second centuries, and the widespread use of manufactured goods in city and country, many being 'luxuries' imported from other parts of the Roman Empire. The main stimulus for this change was because Roman rule required the *civitates* to produce a surplus specifically for the *tributa*, along with a measure more to provide the funds required for the future development of the community itself. In addition the Romans introduced more efficient methods of food production and storage which made it possible to produce the required surplus in the first place, and the means for any residue to be exchanged for other commodities.

The revolution in indigenous farming suggests some sophistry in Strabo's prophecy that any occupation of Britain would materially damage the Roman treasury (*Geog.* 2.5.8). Yet the change was slow, as is revealed by Nero's notion to abandon the province after the Boudiccan Revolt (Suetonius *Nero* 18): he saw it as being of marginal value, in spite of Seneca's heavy investment in its future. Its principal exports remained the same as those noted in Strabo's day: cattle on the hoof, slaves, hunting-dogs, leather, cereals, pearls, gold, silver and iron. Within forty years, however, attitudes had significantly changed. Tacitus notes with great approval the abundance of the island's crop harvests, and other evidence suggests that matters continued to improve in later times. After Constantius saved Britannia for the empire in 296, his achievement was lauded because it 'was a land Rome could not afford to lose – so profuse are its harvests, so numerous the pasturelands, so many the metals to be mined, so profitable the taxes' (Eumenius *Pan.* 11.1).

If we believe these sources, Britannia advanced from a subsistence-based economy to being a major producer of several surplus raw materials essential to the Roman Empire. This in turn, we assume, stimulated overseas trade and the growth of local industries, along with an increase in population size. Then followed the development and expansion of the cities and towns that served the entire process as market centres. Yet, while Britannia now belonged to a world with a developed market and monetary economy, it clearly never ranked among Rome's wealthier provinces. Such is implied by the lack of any British senators at Rome, suggesting that none of Britannia's citizens could satisfy the required 250,000 *denarii* property census for the rank. Likewise, while in every other Roman province inscriptions indicate that public amenities and facilities were often paid for by individuals or groups, similar examples of private munificence in Britannia are conspicuous by their absence. The theatre at Brough-on-Humber, given by Marcus Ulpius Januarius in about 140, is a rare exception that proves the general rule.

The explanation for the conundrum is not that Tacitus and Eumenius have misled us, but that Britannia's most valuable natural assets were effectively monopolised by Rome. Cereals, for example, the best-known of the island's products, were the mainstay of the military diet, and a large part of Britannia's surplus was required to feed the soldiers both on the island and in the European provinces. Consequently, we might deduce from the absence of villas in East Anglia, the major grain-belt of Britannia, that the area was largely imperial land and that much of the grain produced by individuals and the *civitates* was appropriated as *tributum*. As for the island's other main natural resource, its extensive metal deposits, these were owned outright by the emperor and, while leased out to private companies, the imperial exchequer took most of the profits. Of the metals found in Britannia, the most remunerative was lead, as the ore was easy to mine and rich in silver, removed by the cupellation process: the Mendips were being worked for this purpose by AD 49, and British lead-pigs, with their silver extracted, were available at places as far distant as *Pompeii* by AD 79. Other mineral resources were less profitable, but Welsh gold and copper were being extracted on an industrial scale by *c*.100, and it is likely that Cornish tin and Wealden iron were likewise exploited at an early date.

Given that the wealth generated by the exploitation of both cereals and minerals went straight to Rome, it was difficult for either private individuals or the *civitates* to make any significant profit from them. We see clear evidence for this when we examine those urban settlements closely associated with imperial concerns. The *civitas* centre of the Iceni at Caistor-by-Norwich and the *vicus* at Chelmsford, for example, never acquired more than the most basic of urban facilities and amenities and remained quite small throughout their history. As for the *vici* at Charterhouse-on-Mendip and Dolaucothi, both serving mining industries, these remained nothing more than simple villages, despite the wealth they produced, the only amenity known at either being the small amphitheatre provided for the military garrison at Charterhouse.

Yet, away from these imperial enterprises, Roman rule allowed a marked increase in the overall standards of living in Britannia. The economic system that prevailed encouraged a 'trickle-down' process. Surplus wealth generated by private landowners and farmers galvanised commerce and industry, while entrepreneurs ensured that an increasing range of consumer goods was available to the people at large. Some were items that could not be produced locally and were initially imported to satisfy the demands of the garrison: for example, wine and dried fruits, along with olives, olive oil and *garum*, a pungent fish-sauce used equally for flavouring and for disguising the incipient putrefaction of meat in a world lacking cold-storage facilities. Such goods were usually shipped in amphorae, and it is their sherds that testify to the trade for, while pottery vessels are easily broken, the resulting pieces are indestructible, and their exact origins can often be identified from the clays used in their manufacture. Hence, it is possible to demonstrate that immediately after the conquest shiploads of amphorae with a range of perishable comestibles began to arrive in Britannia in increasing numbers, bringing with them smaller cargoes of the better-quality mass-produced ceramics of the Roman world (figure 19).

It is the sherds of these finer wares that provide the evidence for the commercial contacts between Britannia and the remainder of the Roman Empire. Rarely traded in their own right, fine wares were carried as a 'piggy-back' cargo with larger bulk shipments of more profitable goods such as wine and oil. They therefore indicate the overall patterns of Roman trade and, as they can also be closely dated, we can identify the changing patterns of trade. During the late first century BC, for example, wealthy people in the south of England could already obtain the red-gloss pottery known as Arretine Ware, from Tuscany, and after the invasion the similar, if slightly inferior, samian ware (or *terra sigillata*) from South Gaul. Glass, much more highly prized than ceramics, also began to be imported at this time from the same regions and in a wide variety of forms, owing to the recent development of glass-blowing, which made mass-production possible.

Trade routes shifted somewhat between *c*.50 and 100, and Britannia started to receive ceramics from the western Roman Empire, such as Central Gaulish samian ware, *terra rubra*, a polished red-ware from the Lower Rhine, and *terra nigra*, its black counterpart. At the same time, as food prepared according to Roman preferences required that many of the ingredients be first pounded or puréed in a *mortarium*, South and Central Gaul began to export *mortaria* to Britannia. The same regions

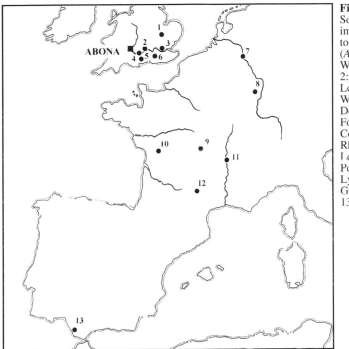

Figure 19.
Sources of imported pottery to Sea Mills (*Abona*). 1: Water Newton; 2: Oxford; 3: London; 4: Wiltshire; 5: Dorset; 6: New Forest; 7: Cologne; 8: Rheinzabern; 9: Lezoux; 10: Poitiers; 11: Lyon; 12: La Graufesenque; 13: Cadiz.

also produced brown- and green-glazed pottery, while Hispania and South Gaul were the origins of two other fine wares popular in first-century Britannia, encrusted cups and thinly potted drinking vessels made from a fine white clay, and aptly known as egg-shell ware. Trade patterns altered again in the second century, with East Gaulish samian ware and then the shiny-black Rhenish Wares becoming common. Finally, during the late fourth century, African red-slip wares from Tunisia begin to appear in Britannia, indicating another shift in trade, although these never became universal in the province, suggesting trade between the two regions was minimal.

Identifying exactly what private surpluses were produced in Britannia to pay for such imports is difficult: hardly surprising, as the literary evidence indicates the majority of traded and exported commodities were of a perishable nature. What there is suggests that privately produced supplies of cereals, hides, livestock, slaves and hunting-dogs continued to play a large part in the island's export trade after the Roman invasion. Salt was certainly a major export and was produced on a near-industrial scale on the east coast in Roman times, and we might assume that some entrepreneur managed to capitalise on the

Roman demand for *radix Britannica*: a dock plant found only in Britain, it was highly esteemed for its medical qualities and was in use by the Roman garrison in Germany in Augustan times. Likewise, the inclusion of British beer in Diocletian's Prices Edict of 301, which set the official prices of goods commonly traded in the Eastern Roman Empire, suggests that it was brewed for export as well as domestic use. British barley-wine, on the other hand, was unlikely to have been exported: it caused 'headaches and bad tempers and is harmful to the nerves' (Dioscorides *De Med. Mat.* 2.88).

To judge from inscriptions, however, Britannia's most valued trading commodity in Roman times was probably wool. A third-century inscription, for example, records how a governor of Britannia sent a *tossia Britannica* to his friend in Gaul. A garment of some kind, it was probably tweed-cloth woven in the coloured checked or striped patterns favoured by the Britons, and the antecedent of the modern-day plaids. While this item was a private gift, it does indicate that British woollen cloths were in demand on the continent, the heavy windproof and waterproof material no doubt being greatly appreciated in the more northerly parts of the Roman Empire (the same regions where modern Harris tweeds are still in great favour for the same qualities). As such, we can understand why an official woollen mill was established in the fourth century 'at *Venta* in Britannia' – probably *Venta Belgarum* (Winchester) – to supply military clothing for the army in the north-western provinces.

The military clothing made at *Venta* was quite different from the *tossia Britannica* or the British woollen goods noted in Diocletian's Prices Edict. These included not only two types of *tapete Britannicum*, a woollen rug, at prices of 4000 and 5000 *denarii* respectively, but also the *birrus Britannicus*, a hooded woollen cloak, sold for 6000 *denarii*. Exact comparisons with modern monetary values are impossible, but the Edict gives us other charges and costs which allow us to put them in some context. An unskilled sewer-man, for example, received 20 *denarii* per day, a barber 2 *denarii* per shave, and a tailor could charge 30 *denarii* for a day's work; a school teacher, on the other hand, earned 40–50 *denarii* each day, while an advocate got 1000 *denarii* per case; finally, the 6000 *denarii* price-tag attached to the *birrus Britannicus* would buy some 300 kg of pork or about 500 litres of the cheapest wine. These woollen goods were therefore very much luxury items and reveal the wider popularity and exclusivity of British-made garments in the Roman Empire, often in spite of any real need for their inherent qualities – just as the Barbour jackets made in North Shields today are as common in sunny Turkey as in rainy Britain!

The main centres for all forms of commercial exchange were the cities and towns, and London and York had extensive warehouses along their riverbanks for the wholesale trade of both import and export items. Retail trade, on the other hand, was generally conducted from simple stalls erected in the relevant centres on regular market days. These itinerant traders usually specialised in a single type of merchandise, as we learn from the debris of a fire that ravaged the *forum-basilica* at Wroxeter one market day *c.* AD 175: among the stalls burnt were those of ironmongers and traders in samian ware. Such stalls were surely usual in the *fora* of the cities on market days, to judge from the number of small coins found trapped amongst the paving stones in areas close to the surrounding colonnades, and we might assume a wide range of luxuries was available, as well as the durables and comestibles for everyday use.

Market stalls apart, more permanent commercial premises were a regular feature in all cities and towns. In some cases these took the form of *macella*, or shopping arcades, as at Cirencester, Leicester and *Verulamium*, although the side rooms of some *fora-basilicae* were also used for this purpose. Much more usual were small shops taking up the street-end of strip-houses or, as at *Verulamium*, single rooms in a block facing on to a main street. Most were retail premises, like the pottery and glass shop identified at Colchester. Some, however, linked production and retail activities in the same building, the front part used for selling goods manufactured in the back. A shop at *Verulamium*, for example, was probably making and selling sausages on the premises, given the type of bone refuse associated with it, another was a metal-working establishment, and a shoemaker's business was carried on in a house just outside the defences of Cirencester, to judge from the large number of hob-nails recovered from the site.

In addition to such service enterprises, epigraphic and archaeological evidence reveals that a large range of commercial manufactories and industries developed in the urban centres of Britannia. Most were evidently small family concerns of the type usual in underdeveloped countries, such as the goldsmiths working in London before AD 60 and at Malton in the third century, silversmiths at Silchester and Leicester, coppersmiths at Colchester and Lincoln, ironsmiths at Chichester, and ironmongers at London. The military *vicus* of Church Brough had a brooch manufactory, as did Caistor-by-Norwich; Bath and Cirencester were home to professional sculptors and monumental masons; the *vicus* at Castleford housed a spoon-maker; Caistor-by-Norwich had a glassworks; and Colchester had a small oil-lamp factory before AD 60.

A few manufactories were on a more industrial scale, supplying goods to a wide range of people or region. In London, for example, there were at least two abattoirs, as well as large bone-working and tanning concerns in the Walbrook area, and fish-sauce was made commercially at Billingsgate. Large imported millstones used in donkey-powered mills attest to wholesale flour merchants and/or bakeries at London, Canterbury, *Verulamium* and Silchester, while Gloucester had its own municipal tilery, and private brickworks existed at London, Wroxeter and Alcester. In the same vein were the at least six different 'schools' of mosaicists working in Britannia, two based at Cirencester, and one each at Dorchester, Water Newton, Brough-on-Humber, and (probably) Winchester: they reached their apogee in the fourth century, the Cirencester schools being especially successful, with over fifty mosaics to their credit in Britannia, and one in Germany.

Industries of this type, while no doubt profitable for their owners, nonetheless usually served a fairly localised market. Two of the manufacturing industries in Britannia, however, did develop during the third and fourth centuries to become of greater than local importance. The less studied of the two is the pewtering industry, although three main centres are known, one close to Bath, the others at Camerton and Nettleton Scrub. Pewter, an alloy of lead and tin, can be polished to produce a surface gloss which is close to that of silver. Moreover, while hard to work as a sheet metal, it can be easily cast in moulds to produce bowls, platters, flagons, pitchers and the like – even pocket-size portable shrines for the particularly devout! As a result, once lead-mining was effectively privatised in the third century, pewter became widely used to produce imitations of the more expensive silver prototypes, the accessibility of the necessary raw materials in the province allowing its ready production on an extensive scale for internal trade and for export to Gaul and Germany.

Much more is known of the other major manufacturing industry of Britannia, the pottery trade. In the early Roman period most pottery was made only in sufficient quantity locally to supply the nearest urban centre. A rare exception to this rule was the black-burnished wares produced in south-west England and in Essex during the second and third centuries, and mainly found on military sites in the north of England, suggesting a military monopoly. That apart, by the third and fourth centuries a number of potteries in other parts of England had developed on such a scale that they can properly be called industries, even if they were mainly rural, to minimise public nuisance and maximise resources and transport systems. The potteries of the Oxford region, for example, of mainly late-third-century date, were roughly equidistant from Cirencester, Silchester, *Verulamium* and Leicester, each a *civitas* centre. Similarly, the later New Forest potteries had ready access to London, Silchester, Winchester and Chichester, the last two also being the centres

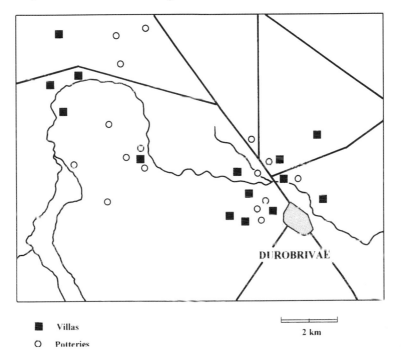

Villas

Potteries

2 km

Figure 20. Potteries and villas in the vicinity of Water Newton (*Durobrivae*).

of *civitates*. A clear idea of the potential profits to be generated by this industry is provided by the case of the *vicus* at Water Newton, in the Nene valley. Here, the availability of good clays and access to markets in the north and south, by road or by river and the North Sea, accelerated its development to such an extent that by the third century it was surrounded by many potteries and several villas (figure 20). Indeed, the *vicus* itself had grown so large that its walled area, at 18 ha, was some 4 ha bigger than that of Caistor-by-Norwich, the official administrative centre of its *civitas*, while walled area and suburbs combined, at 100 ha, matched the walled area of London.

Yet, despite the positive tone adopted here, we might retain the same doubts as Strabo about the Roman occupation of Britain: was it ever a positive contributor to the overall economy of the Roman Empire? To an extent, this is the wrong question to ask: the classical world did not have the globalising trends apparent today. Moreover, Rome was never a truly imperialist or colonialist state and did not have to satisfy the economic concerns of modern nations. Even so, in general it expected the provinces to cover their own expenses, and we can doubt if this was ever possible in Britannia simply because of the size of its garrison. At full strength in the early second century, it was the largest in terms of the territory it controlled, with some 50,000 men in all, or 13.8 per cent of the entire Roman army: by comparison, all Asia Minor and the Near East, some three times greater in area and much more heavily populated, was garrisoned by about 78,000 soldiers, or 21.4 per cent of the total army strength. At an annual cost of not less that 20 million *denarii* in pay alone, a quantity of silver equivalent to £11,200,000 in 2001, one might question if Britannia ever returned sufficient in money taxes to pay for it, stressing the importance of the *tributum* in kind to maintain this force.

It would be naïve to assert that Rome would not have continued to occupy the island unless a substantial portion of these costs were returned in local taxes: Rome did, after all, sometimes abandon territories which were not economically viable, as when Hadrian gave up Trajan's eastern conquests. Yet we should remember that Nero did consider quitting Britannia at the time of the Boudiccan Revolt and was persuaded not to do so only because of the loss of prestige involved. He evidently doubted that continued occupation would ever return the money needed to pay for its garrison and retained the island simply because of its status as the most alien of Rome's provinces, the only one outside the 'known world', and visible proof, therefore, of Rome's destiny to rule without limit. Roman control was thus to be maintained for internal and external prestige, no matter how much it cost.

5
Religion and religious buildings

The religion of Britannia, like most of the classical world, was pantheistic, no single belief having official precedence until Theodosius I elevated Christianity to the rank in 395. People accepted the existence of several natural and supernatural forces that affected all aspects of everyday life, and that certain superhuman and semi-divine entities, the 'gods', directed these forces. Consequently, no one dogma or doctrine could be consistently applied to any religion in the Roman Empire, the monotheistic cults of Judaism and, later, Christianity apart. Similarly, with few exceptions, all religions were universally tolerated, only Druidism being banned, as it involved human sacrifice. There was no trained or official priesthood, the priests responsible for supervising a community's religious affairs being appointed as a form of social honour.

Indeed, it was the lack of a single unifying belief in the Roman world that resulted in the imperial cult, a quasi-religious doctrine most Roman subjects acknowledged. It was officially instituted in the western provinces after Augustus became *pontifex maximus*, chief priest of Rome, in 12 BC. As senior mediator between Rome and all of the gods, it gave him the power to impose an obligation that each citizen make regular oaths of loyalty and dedicate sacrifices to him, for his part in securing the good favour of the gods for all public and private enterprises. Consequently, the imperial cult developed into an essential part of Roman provincial administration, responsibility for its maintenance being assigned to the provincial councils. Even so, the principal centres of the cult were always established in the *coloniae* and *municipia* of a province rather than its *civitas* centres. This was because of its specifically Roman nature, embodying the emperor's position as *pontifex maximus*. On the other hand, it was usual for the six priests (*seviri Augustales*) in each centre to be chosen from the prominent traders of the community, many of them freedmen and otherwise denied a place in local political life, as magisterial office was restricted to freeborn citizens. By this method, successful and wealthy freedmen could play a significant part in their own community and give their families the prestige for their sons to try for political office with an improved chance of success, despite being the descendants of former slaves.

In Britannia the principal centre for the imperial cult was at Colchester, where a sacred complex for the purpose was begun in about AD 55. It was a colonnaded enclosure, or *templum*, with an *aedes*, or shrine, and an altar, or *ara*. As Graeco-Roman religion emphasised public sacrifice and not closed congregational worship, the *ara* was the focus of all ceremonial, the *aedes*, the building we call the temple, being merely a symbolic home for the deity, and never intended for group worship. That apart, the imperial *aedes* at Colchester was one of the very few Roman-style religious buildings in Britannia. It stood on a barrel-vaulted podium (still visible beneath the Norman castle built above it) measuring some 32 by 24.5 metres and 4 metres high and was reached by a wide stairway. The façade incorporated a pedimented porch, some 9 metres high, supported on eight Corinthian columns at the front and two on the sides, with access through a high doorway into the *cella*, the closed part of the *aedes*. This was bare of fixed furnishings other than a statue of Claudius and images of Roma and Victory, to celebrate the conquest of Britain. It was, however, used to store the gifts dedicated to the cult and, as a place protected by the gods, also as a treasury for the community and individual citizens, thus making it seem to the contemporary viewer more like a warehouse than a place of awe and devotion.

The Roman conquest also brought the indigenous population closer to the Olympian gods, and especially the principal gods of Rome itself: Jupiter, Juno and Minerva, the Capitoline Triad. Those communities which directly benefited from Roman rule eagerly promoted these deities, as at *Verulamium*, where the *aedes* in the *forum-basilica* was probably a *capitolium*, a shrine to the Capitoline Triad, as appropriate for a *municipium Romanum*. Likewise, such buildings of Graeco-Roman type exist at Wroxeter, which probably had a large veteran community, and Corbridge, first a military *vicus* and later a *civitas* capital. Other classical deities and cults were popularised by those who supported Roman rule, for example Cogidubnus, king of the Regni, who authorised an *aedes* for Neptune and Minerva at Chichester, while elsewhere in the province classical gods were introduced by legionary and auxiliary soldiers, and by officials and traders now active in the island. Thus dedications to Mars as god of war have been found in the military regions of the province, while Mercury, patron deity of trade, was venerated in commercial centres such as London.

Apart from Colchester and *Verulamium*, however, shrines of Graeco-Roman type, presumably dedicated to the worship of the Olympian deities, are found only at Wroxeter and Corbridge, although one formed the focus of the sanctuary of Sulis-Minerva at Bath. Instead, it appears that most of Britannia's shrines dedicated to the classical deities consisted of an enclosed *templum* and *ara*, without an *aedes*. Such a setting can be envisaged for London's 'Screen of the Gods', a large altar of *c.*275, with reliefs of the Olympian pantheon, later demolished for use in the city's third-century riverside defences. Clearly it was once the focus of a large public square, enclosed by a wall and entered by the similarly decorated archway whose remains were also reused in these defences.

Shrines to purely classical deities being rare in Britannia, the practice of syncretism, or fusion, was much more usual in spreading knowledge of them among the native population. Once the individual 'power' and 'influence' of an indigenous deity were known, it could be matched to a classical equivalent. In this way, the British Andate was identified as the Roman Victoria, both being goddesses of military victory, and Sulis was assimilated with the Roman Minerva, as patron deities of craftwork, even though Sulis also had a strong healing aspect. As a result, while a few Celtic gods retained a distinct indigenous identity, as with Epona, goddess of horses, most were paired with a Roman god and appear with 'double-barrelled' names. Typical is Mars Cocidius, in which Cocidius, the 'Red One', was revered as a local version of Mars, as a god of war; another example is Jupiter Loucetius, where Loucetius, the 'Brilliant One', was equated with Jupiter, as both are thunder-gods.

The deities of pre-Roman Britain, however, were mainly connected with the powers of nature and usually venerated in the open air, in groves or at springs. A sanctuary of this type was known as a *nemeton*, and it sometimes contained a circular timber house as a 'home' for the spirit or spirits honoured there. After the Roman conquest many such timber shrines were replaced with stone buildings of so-called Romano-Celtic type, in which a circular, rectangular or polygonal *cella* was surrounded by a colonnaded ambulatory. As might be expected, most examples are found in rural contexts, and some subsequently developed into 'temple-towns', as with Bath and Buxton, the other 'spa town' of Britannia, whose Roman name – *Aquae Arnemetiae* – is derived from the word *nemeton*. Another example is Nettleton Scrub, a pre-Roman sanctuary of the gods Cunomaglos and Rosmerta: he was equated with Apollo, while she maintained her Celtic identity, and the sanctuary subsequently developed into a major temple-town with the addition of shrines to Silvanus, Mercury and Diana, among other deities.

Despite their predominantly rural location, some Romano-Celtic shrines are found in some *civitas* centres, perhaps preserving the site of a pre-Roman *nemeton*. This allows for the possibility that – as at Trier (*Augusta Treverorum*) – these locations were chosen for urban development by Roman officials as they already fulfilled a recognised religious, political and social function. It was probably so at Silchester, where a pre-Roman *nemeton* may be the origin of an *insula* in the east part of the town: not only does it contain at least two Romano-Celtic shrines, but it is directly linked to the *forum-basilica* by a road which may well have been a formal processional way. More usually, however, urban shrines of Romano-Celtic type are found within an otherwise undifferentiated part of a regular *insula*. Such is the case with the other three Romano-Celtic shrines at Silchester, although elsewhere they do

50

Figure 21. The Romano-Celtic temple at Caerwent (see also plate 12).

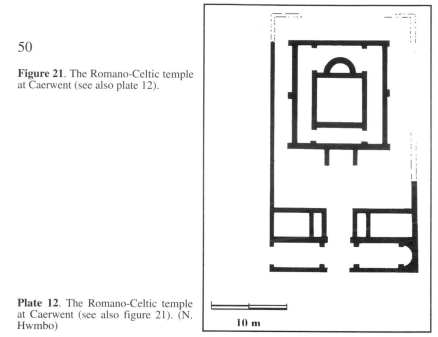

Plate 12. The Romano-Celtic temple at Caerwent (see also figure 21). (N. Hwmbo)

10 m

Plate 13. An inscription recording a temple of Serapis at York. (Yorkshire Museum)

sometimes occupy a prominent position in the urban topography. At Caerwent, for example, the *insula* immediately west of the *forum-basilica* was cleared in the late third century for the construction of a Romano-Celtic shrine (figure 21 and plate 12).

In the late second century new religious beliefs of oriental origin became popular in the Roman Empire. They shared a common characteristic in being usually restricted to men of some social status, who underwent exotic and secret initiation rites in return for eternal salvation. Because of the secrecy surrounding these rites, often orgiastic and hysterical in character, they are known as the 'mystery cults'. Most popular were those of the Egyptian deities Isis and Osiris/Serapis, and the Phrygian Cybele and her mortal consort Attis. Inscriptions inform us that by *c*.200 there were cult centres to Isis at London and to Osiris/Serapis at York (plate 13), while *dendrophori*, officials of the cult of Cybele, are recorded at *Verulamium*. Moreover, a pair of elaborately decorated ceremonial pincers found in the Thames at London seem to be ritual castration tongs associated with a shrine of Cybele: new priests of the cult were emasculated, in imitation of Attis's self-mutilation to foil an arranged marriage to another mortal and stress his devotion to Cybele.

In the mid third century two new oriental cults spread throughout the Roman Empire. The first was Mithraism, a branch of Persian Zoroastrianism, whose followers saw the world in terms of an eternal struggle between the powers of good (light) and evil (darkness), and who believed that Mithras mediated on man's behalf, killing the primeval bull to release its blood (energy) for the benefit of mankind. The cult, restricted to men only, offered its disciples an eventual escape from the 'darkness' of mortal existence into the 'lightness' of eternal life after death – but only in return for total subjugation and commitment: hence the separate initiation rites for the seven levels of devotion, some involving a symbolic burial and resurrection through the use of bull's blood. Indeed, it was this emphasis on commitment, courage and honesty that made it particularly attractive to army officers and the more wealthy traders. Thus the cult shrines, or *mithraea*, are well represented in the military areas and commercial centres of the Empire, the largest in Britannia being at London, the major trading centre on the island. It is typical of the type: an aisled hall with raised side-benches for the initiates, and the necessary burial pit next to the door, with an apse at the far end dominated by a sculpture of Mithras slaughtering the bull. To simulate the cave in which this event took place, the building was partly sunk into the ground and had few windows, these being set high up in the nave for ventilation rather than illumination.

The second of the new mystery cults which became popular during the third century was Christianity. It also laid an emphasis on eternal salvation for those who endured a ceremonial rebirth, after which the believer could participate in its other rituals, especially the transubstantiation, an observance involving procedures and beliefs quite alien to classical theology. What gave Christianity its greater popularity over the other mystery religions, and its eventual success as the single official religion in the Roman Empire, was St Paul's astute resolve to open the doctrine to all, no matter what their original faith, sex or social class. It established the sect as a separate religion from Judaism, which limited membership on matrilineal lines, and naturally appealed to the vast majority of people who were refused admission to the other mystery cults because of their sex or because they lacked sufficient wealth and social standing.

On the other hand, Christianity denied the divinity of the emperor and the power of the Roman gods, disavowing these stable factors in everyday life in favour of one Jesus Christ, whom the Romans adjudged a legally executed criminal. As a result, early Christians were often considered heretical and sometimes became the target of pogroms, especially as many prided themselves in goading their fellow citizens by proselytising and refusing to swear oaths in the name of the emperor. Despite such provocative displays of lèse-majesté, however, the religion was rarely the target of official persecution, for the majority of Christians – as with the Jews of the Diaspora – were careful to maintain a low profile in their own communities. Thus most early 'churches' were private houses converted to form a communion hall and baptistery, and not prominent purpose-built buildings. Such *domi ecclesiasticae* are known in Palestine, Syria and Rome, but no urban examples have yet been found in Britannia, although they are known in rural contexts, as in the villas at Lullingstone, Frampton and Hinton St Mary.

It seems highly likely that Christianity was not widespread in Britannia until after the Edict of Milan in 313, when it was formally recognised as

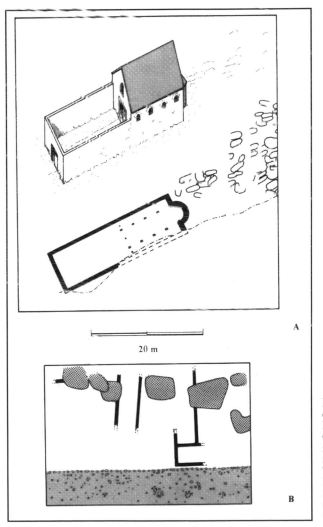

20 m

A

B

Figure 22. (A) The cemetery church at Butt Road, Colchester: plan and restored view (see also plate 14). (B) The decline of Roman Canterbury: Saxon huts and pits cutting into Roman walls.

Plate 14. The cemetery church at Butt Road, Colchester (see also figure 22A). (N. Hwmbo)

of equal status with all other religions in the Roman world. For example, whereas *Ancyra* in Asia Minor alone had some twelve named martyrs in the official persecutions of Decius in 250, and of Diocletian and Galerius in 303–11, the whole of Britannia provided exactly three: Alban at *Verulamium*, and Aaron and Julius at Caerleon. True, the bishops of York, London and Lincoln attended the Council of Arles in 314, along with a delegation probably from Colchester, suggesting some form of episcopal organisation based on the four provinces then existing in Britannia. Even so, the sparse references to Christianity in Britannia in the Roman period are generally concerned with disputes over dogma. Other than revealing that the British church shared in the religious controversies of the fourth and fifth centuries, they tell us nothing about the popularity of the religion itself.

Hard material evidence for Christian congregations in Britannia is scarce, and generally comes from the countryside and the *vici*, suggesting it gained its greatest number of converts from the rural poor. It usually takes the form of graffiti or small portable objects with Christian emblems, the remarkable hoard of communion silver found at Water Newton and the lead 'baptism' tanks from East Anglia being rare exceptions to the rule. There are no certain traces of the urban churches implied by the existence of bishops at London, York and Lincoln, although a building at Butt Road, Colchester, may well be such a structure (figure 22A and plate 14). It has the basilical plan and eastern apse common in early Roman churches and is associated with graves aligned in the same direction, as usual with Christian burials. However, it should perhaps be interpreted as a cemetery chapel rather than a congregational church, even though such buildings more usually took the form of *martyria*. These were the simple shrines constructed over the graves of celebrated martyrs, and a likely example is the late-Roman building that forms the basis of St Martin's, Canterbury. These structures apart, the clearest evidence for Christianity in Britannia is the cemetery excavated at Poundbury, Dorchester, discussed in the next chapter.

6
Urban society in Roman Britain

Our direct knowledge of Roman-British urban society is limited. To begin with, we do not even know how large the urban population was. According to Tacitus, who perhaps used official census returns, some 70,000 people were killed at London, Colchester and *Verulamium* in the Boudiccan Revolt (Tacitus *Ann.* 14.33). If not an exaggeration, and accepting the figure probably included casualties from the rural *territoria* as well, we might suppose that London at the time had a population of about 15,000, the other cities some 7000 each. On the other hand, an estimate based on the areas enclosed by the third-century defences found at most Roman-British cities (figure 1) and their apparent density of occupation suggests that by that time London had a population of about 30,000; Cirencester and Wroxeter perhaps 20,000 inhabitants apiece; the other cities around 7000; and an 'average' *vicus* some 3500. In very broad terms, the urban population of third-century Britannia was about 550,000. It was greatly outnumbered by the population of the countryside, which the latest estimates place at about 2,500,000. While no claims of precision are made for these figures they are close to what we know of the population of early medieval Britain, when climate and density of settlement were comparable, suggesting they are reasonably accurate.

Some of those who lived in Roman Britain were notable personalities according to inscriptions and occasional literary references. While much of this information concerns the officials who came to Britannia on assignment, a few nonetheless deserve mention for their part in the urbanisation of the province. A term of office in Britannia was a common stage in the career of many Roman citizens of distinction, and the island was often temporary home to some of the ablest executives in the Roman Empire. Among them is the best-known of Britannia's governors, Gaius Julius Agricola, a native of Fréjus (*Forum Julii*) in Gallia Narbonensis, renowned for extending Roman domination into Caledonia. The eulogy written by his son-in-law, Tacitus, reveals a man who fully understood his responsibilities as a governor and used his personal authority and resources to expedite the urbanisation of Britannia (see Chapter 2).

Next in importance to the governor, and of almost equal consequence in the way the island became 'Roman', was the imperial procurator. Personally chosen by the emperor to oversee financial matters and imperial property in the province, he was quite independent of the governor, which meant that many procurators wielded great authority in provincial matters – some for better, a few for worse. Of the latter, one of the least reputable was Decianus Catus, whose actions after the death of King Prausutagus initiated the Boudiccan Revolt. Of the former, one of the most humane was Julius Alpinus Classicianus, Catus's immediate successor. A man of Gaulish origin, he won regard by mitigating the harsh treatment of the Britons demanded by Suetonius Paulinus, who was governor at the time. He died while still in office and was buried in London, a magnificent funerary altar being erected in his honour by his wife, Julia Pacata Indiana.

Agricola, Catus and Classicianus were but three of many Roman citizens of varying origins dispatched from Rome to serve in the provincial administration of Britannia. Among others who deserve mention are Gaius Octavius Iavolenus Priscus, from *Nedinum*, Dalmatia, *legatus iuridicus* (legal advisor to the governor) in the mid second century and later governor of Africa, one of the two premier posts available to a senator. Another was Gnaeus Munatius Aurelius Bassus from *Nomentum*, Latium (plate 1), *censitor* (census officer) of Roman citizens in Colchester in the early second century and later prefect of the imperial works office at Rome. A third was Titus Haterius Nepos, from *Fulginium*, Umbria, appointed by Trajan as *censitor* of the Anavionenses of Annandale in order to assess their due *tributum*, the first stage of a distinguished career which included being procurator of Armenia Major and ended with the successive posts of prefect of the Vigiles at Rome and prefect of Egypt, the highest positions open to a man of his status

As such men came to Britannia in an official capacity, with no choice in the matter, of greater interest are those who chose to arrive and settle on the island of their own volition, even if on a temporary basis. Indeed, given that an assignment to Britannia was held in contempt amongst the self-elected cultural élite of Roman society – 'I would not like to have to walk among the Britons', wrote Florus (*Hist. Aug. Hadrian* 16.3) – these men are much more worthy of investigation. It should come as no surprise, however, that many of the migrants who came to Britannia were entrepreneurs of one kind or another. Even so, by their origins and trades, they reveal how Roman imperialism allowed a greater degree of social and ethnic mobility than had ever existed before – or perhaps since. For example, among a long list of non-official migrants who worked, settled and sometimes died in Britannia we might mention Priscus, a Gaulish sculptor who worked at Bath; the Palmyrene Barates, a flag-maker on Hadrian's Wall, who married his ex-slave Regina, a woman of British origin; and Mantios, a *mulomedicus* or mule-doctor, from the Greek-speaking eastern Empire, who was buried near Taplow. One of the more interesting was Demetrius of Tarsus, a professional teacher of Greek, and compatriot and near contemporary of St Paul, as well as acquaintance of Plutarch. While in Britannia he was 'requested' by the emperor Domitian to explore and report on the Hebrides and evidently did not relish the experience. On his return he set up dedications at York to several deities, including Oceanus, before thankfully taking a less arduous appointment in the eastern Empire.

One thing that made such migration possible was the universality of Roman rule. It allowed freedom of movement within an empire that controlled the entire known world. The other factor was the universality of Latin, the *lingua franca* of the time. While Greek was more usual in the eastern parts of the Roman Empire, as well as the second language of all who thought themselves true world citizens, Latin was the major means of communication in all areas and essential for anyone who desired advancement, whatever their mother tongue. For example, Barates, our Syrian flag-maker, was probably most at ease when speaking Palmyrene, his native dialect. Yet, while he would have been familiar with Greek, the usual vernacular in Syria, and probably knew British Celtic (assuming he did talk with his wife), he presumably also spoke Latin, the official speech of the army garrisons he was selling flags to.

To what extent Roman-British urban society in general adopted Latin as a regular means of communication cannot be accurately assessed. The local British Celtic evidently remained in regular use in rural areas, for it 'borrowed' Latin words for new artefacts and challenging intellectual concepts, especially those associated with agriculture: hence certain of the Latinisms in Welsh and Cornish. However, as no written records in British Celtic survive from the Roman period, it would appear this language was restricted to the least literate sections of society, unlike Gaulish Celtic, occasionally written down with Latin or Greek letters.

On the other hand a widespread knowledge and use of Latin among the citizens of Britannia may be assumed, as implied by Gildas, the sixth-century British historian – and ardent moralist and loyalist – who referred to Latin as *nostra lingua*, 'our language'. Indeed, from a variety of evidence we might conclude that a reasonable level of fluency was usual – fluency, in this sense, meaning the use of a language on a regular and entirely natural basis, not simply a command of the grammar and a working vocabulary. Such is indicated by Tacitus's scathing comment, 'In place of a distaste for the Latin tongue came a passion to command it' (*Agr.* 21). There is certainly enough evidence for schooling and some degree of education among the upper classes of Britannia. Professional teachers, like Demetrius of Tarsus, are well attested, while *styli*, used for writing on wax tablets, have been found in most towns, as have inkwells and ink-pens, although the few fragments of parchment and wooden writing tablets which have survived in urban contexts are normally official in character.

A better indicator of the extent to which Latin was used in everyday life is given by the few advertisements which have survived, as they imply a functional literacy at least among the population. A good example is the painted motto on a *mortarium* from Water Newton, informing us that 'Sennianus of *Durobrivae*' made it. Most surviving painted advertisements, however, are found on imported amphorae and indicate their contents, one example from London recording these as 'Lucius Tettius Africanus's superior fish-sauce from *Antipolis* (Antibes)', another naming them as 'green olives'. A general level of functional literacy is also suggested by the many pharmacists' stamps that exist, used to indicate the nature of a prescribed medication. From them we learn of such remedies as 'Lucius Julius Juvenis's anti-itching lotion', 'Gaius Valerius Valentinus's celandine paste for inflamed eyes', 'Atticus's poppy unguent for all pains' (presumably opium-based), and – with an appealing lack of modesty – 'Titus Vindacius Ariovistus's infallible balm'.

Best of all evidence for functional literacy in Britannia are the graffiti which have survived. Simple names and the like excepted – as with the graffito from Leicester which gives us the names of Verecunda, a prostitute or actress, and her lover, the gladiator Lucius – these usually idle scribblings indicate the generality of Latin in everyday use. Quite simply, the more transient a record and the greater its obsession with personal matters, the better it indicates general fluency and literacy – especially so if we fail to grasp the exact relevance or purpose of the message! Such messages from the past exist in a variety of forms, if often of a kind familiar in modern life: at Leicester, for example, someone scratched several Latin obscenities on the wall of one house. Of greater interest and value, however, are the often aimless messages written with finger or stick on tiles and the like as they were drying before being fired. Many are likely to be the comments of the workmen themselves, such as that from London which bears the intriguing record that 'Austalis has been disappearing alone every day for thirteen days', while one from Binchester declares how 'Armea has taught me to say "no thanks" to all others'. More certain evidence of literate (and bored?) workmen is a graffito from Leicester which announces that 'Primus made 60 [tiles] just like this'; and two from Silchester, one stating that 'Clementius made this tile'; the other with the single word *satis* – 'Enough!'. Other examples, however, seem to have been used for impromptu writing lessons, such as the tile from Caerwent with the name 'Bellicanus' written on it in at least four different hands, and another from Silchester, used to instruct someone in the alphabet. Of quite uncertain purpose is one more Silchester tile graffito which begins with a list of people whom the writer considered 'untrustworthy', and concludes in the same hand with the opening phrase from Virgil's *Aeneid* Book 2 – 'all fell silent'.

Most numerous of all the Latin inscriptions to survive, however, are the tombstones of those citizens wealthy enough to afford one. Roman law demanded that the dead be buried outside the formal limits of a settlement, and the cemeteries found along the roads leading to and from a community often have tombstones serving as a *memento mori*, as much for the passer-by as for the family involved. Some were simple gabled slabs, bearing a text naming the person(s) memorialised, and the salient features of birth, life and career, although they often also include the names of family and friends who survived them. Others were more elaborate in form, the inscription coming at the foot of an ornate monument, with a carved and painted relief of the person(s) they honoured. The epitaphs themselves, while often fairly standardised, sometimes provide moving demonstrations of family love and care, as with this message from Quintus Corellius Fortis of York: 'For Corellia Optata, aged thirteen … I the father of a virtuous daughter, the victim of unfair hope, pitiably bewail her final end.' While addresses of this kind are rare, they reveal how tombstones are of some value in assessing mortality rates, even if the data cannot be used in a truly scientific way, being limited to a small élite, rather than recording the population at large. Even so, we learn that of this particular class those who survived infancy often died in their early teens; of those who reached maturity many died aged twenty-six to forty-five; very few reached, never mind exceeded, sixty-three, the age the Romans considered the 'great climacteric'.

The methods and types of burials themselves provide an even more personal view of how the urban Roman British contemplated death. In the first and second centuries the dead were often cremated using an *ustrina*, a hollow reserved for the purpose at the cemetery, as at Trentholme Drive in York. The ashes were then sorted and buried in a container, usually a glass or pottery jar, although metal and wooden boxes, and bags of leather or cloth, have also been identified. Burial goods for the afterlife were common, varying from everyday items such as boots, toys, clothes and jewellery to imported and local pottery vessels, often with some food for the long journey to come, while a coin was sometimes provided to pay Charon the ferryman for the journey across the Styx to Hades. It seems that very few graves had any form of permanent marker, although some members of the surviving local aristocracies evidently wished to assert their Celtic heritage by being buried beneath substantial barrows, as at Bartlow and Stevenage.

For uncertain reasons, a gradual change from cremation to inhumation began in about 150, and it became the usual rite by the fourth century, although cremations remained popular in some areas, as at Winchester. While the direct stimulus for the change is unknown, it was probably a shift in popular beliefs about the physical state required of a person to enter the afterlife, a transition that also apparently dictated that the corpse be buried with the head usually towards the north. It did not, however, impose a feeling of sanctity for those already buried, as their graves were often cut by later burials. Grave goods continued to be provided and, while most people were inhumed without a coffin, those who could afford it were buried in a casket of some kind, ranging from a simple wooden box to stone and lead sarcophagi, some of the last being packed with gypsum in an attempt to preserve the body intact throughout eternity. The eastern custom of burial in ornate sarcophagi, exposed to view above ground or within a *hypogeum*, a subterranean chamber, was rare in Britannia, although an example of the latter has been found at York.

Another modification in burial customs appears towards the mid fourth century, the practice of inhuming people with their head to the west. Such graves are almost always without any evidence for burial goods, the few found generally being of personal rather than practical value, as with rings and brooches. In addition, the cemeteries of this type that have been identified – notably at Poundbury, Chichester, and at Butt Road, Colchester – are always well ordered, successive graves almost never cutting into earlier burials. These features are normal practice in Christian cemeteries, reflecting the belief that the deceased will arise in complete physical form to face the dawn on the Day of Judgement and then enter paradise, where the items of this world are not needed.

More accurate – and often exciting – insights into the nature of the urban populations of Britannia are provided by examining their actual buried remains. Indeed, in a sense, archaeologists have equal rights with pathologists to the maxim *mortui viventes docent* – 'the dead teach the living'. From skeletal relics we can learn much about the demography of past societies, the aches and pains of those who lived in earlier times, sometimes even the cause of death or something about an individual's way of life. It needs to be noted, however, that the amount of data available from such analysis for the towns of Britannia is fractional. A mere 3500 burials or so have been scientifically excavated and studied, mainly at London, Winchester, York, Colchester and Dorchester, and yet we might calculate that the total number of urban burials involved for the four hundred years of Roman rule was in the order of eight million. Even so, the results of the research are generally consistent in many ways. For example, the mean heights of the people buried at the different cemeteries did not significantly vary, females in the range

1.57–1.63 metres (5 feet 2 inches to 5 feet 4 inches), and males 1.71–1.80 metres (5 feet 7 inches to 5 feet 11 inches). Likewise, we find that on average some 22 per cent of the population died before they were twenty years old; about 50 per cent in the age range twenty to fifty; and almost all of the remainder before they were seventy. The figures are comparable to those found in the urban settlements of many underdeveloped countries today, in which living conditions are hard, disease and infection are rife, and nutrition and medical care are inadequate.

As it is, examination of the skeletal remains from urban Roman-British cemeteries clearly demonstrates that life was indeed harder than we would accept, given the choice. Dental caries and osteoarthritis, for example, were relatively common by the age of thirty-five, and most principal joints show evidence of wear and tear. Fractures were also a relatively universal pathological condition, more so than now: most had healed well, including the sixteen or so rib-fractures a man at Cirencester occasioned in his lifetime! Higher levels of lead than are acceptable today are seen in several individuals buried at London and Cirencester, a result, presumably, of using lead or pewter vessels for food preparation rather than consuming water from lead pipes, as lead-piped water supplies were rare in Britannia. Tuberculosis, spina bifida, poliomyelitis, varicose veins and gout all leave their marks on the human skeleton and are recorded on individuals at London, Dorchester and York, but there are no indications of complaints such as rickets or venereal disease, both of which leave some evidence on the skeleton.

It is also clear that the people of Britannia were prone to the types of infections and diseases which affect those living in underdeveloped societies, but which leave no mark on the skeleton. Documentary evidence suggests that trachoma and other eye infections disabled as much as 20 per cent of the Roman-British garrison on occasion, and the urban population probably suffered in equal proportion, given that the majority of pharmacist's stamps are for eye ointments. Trachoma is a viral disease transmitted by flies and indicates unsanitary living conditions made worse by a lack of vitamins A and C: the remains of fleas and human lice from many Roman-British urban rubbish-pits – and finds of latrine-fly pupae at London, pubic lice from Carlisle, and bedbugs from Alcester – confirm that unhygienic conditions were not unknown in Britannia. Tapeworm has been identified from a solidified cyst in a skeleton from rural Cambridgeshire and was quite probably common in the urban settlements, given the open latrines and sewers.

Skeletal evidence for invasive surgery to fight these and other medical conditions is, however, rare, one of the few examples being a healed trepanned skull from York, indicating a successful operation to relieve pressure on the brain. Surgery was nonetheless common in Britannia, to judge from the discovery of a wide range of surgical tools, including scalpels, artery forceps, a retractor and an abortion probe, none of which differs greatly from its modern equivalent. The lack of skeletal evidence for invasive operations suggests a high level of competence among these early surgeons.

Although the dead teach the living, it is only in very rare cases that they can talk to us direct and explain their manner of death. Quite simply, most events which result in the death of an individual leave little or no evidence on the skeleton and, where such evidence is present, it usually indicates some form of violent death. This was the case of a man buried in the Brunswick Road cemetery at Gloucester, killed by a blow to the head with a blunt instrument, severe enough to drive bone fragments into his brain; and at Housesteads, where a broken sword-tip was found in the ribs of a man buried with a woman beneath the floor of a building in the *vicus*. Murder most foul must also be suspected for the two adults and a decapitated child found buried in disused quarry pits at Sea Mills, and the two soldiers buried one over the other in a single grave at Canterbury, both with their weapons and other equipment. These individuals apart, we can only assume that the vast majority of people in the towns of Britannia died of the usual 'natural' causes, a view supported by the similarity between their mortality rates and those of many modern Third World countries.

7
Change and transformation

The increasing popularity of mystery cults such as Mithraism and Christianity in the third century was due to the promise of eternal salvation in a world gradually losing stability. The catalyst was the death of Commodus in 193 and the ensuing four years of civil war. One contender for the imperial throne was Albinus, governor of Britannia, who stripped the island of its troops to campaign in Gaul but was killed at Lyon in 197, leaving Septimius Severus undisputed ruler of Rome. Political stability was thus restored to the Empire as a whole but, in the meantime, the military situation in Britannia had significantly deteriorated, and in 208 Severus arrived on the island in person to prosecute a war against the tribes of Caledonia.

Severus's North British War lasted until his death at York, in 211. By then he had initiated a division of the island into two new provinces, Britannia Inferior and Britannia Superior – in order, we can assume, to forestall any future rebellion. York and London became their official administrative centres, each with the status of a Roman *colonia*, although by this time the rank was devoid of any real advantage, conferred more for social cachet than any legal benefit. Quite simply, the number of full Roman citizens in Britannia – as elsewhere – had grown exponentially since AD 43, and much of its population, especially in the urban centres, would have been citizens from birth. Indeed, that the distinction between Roman citizen and native had now ceased to have any real meaning was recognised by Caracalla's *constitutio Antoniniana* of 212, extending Roman citizenship to all freeborn people in the Empire who lacked it. Henceforth, all provincial communities adopted Roman law, and earlier distinctions in urban status lost their formal purpose.

Yet while in legal terms the urbanisation of Britannia was now complete, it was also now that its cities and towns started to feel the effects of an Empire-wide period of economic decline. After Commodus reduced the silver content of the *denarius* in 180 to support his profligacy, matters worsened during the civil war of 193–7, as rival contenders ravished provincial treasuries to pay their armies. The shortfall of ready cash for everyday use led to periodic debasements of the coinage and a sharp rise in inflation, the first such episode of any significance since Augustus reformed the Roman monetary system in *c*.23 BC. When Severus significantly debased the silver coinage in 196, confidence was further reduced, encouraging more inflation. Matters were not helped when Caracalla devalued the silver standard once more in 215, but any residual faith which remained in the monetary system was soon lost in the rebellions that dominated the Roman Empire in the early third century.

These rebellions began with the murder of Severus Alexander in 235, and before 284, when Diocletian restored stability, no less than twenty-six individuals had claimed the imperial purple. Britannia fortunately escaped any direct involvement during this fifty-year period but in 286 Carausius, commander of the British fleet, declared himself ruler of Britannia and North Gaul. Driven from Gaul in 293, he was replaced by his finance minister Allectus, who continued to rule the island for three more years until Constantius restored the situation. Another reform of the island's administration followed: Britannia Superior was now divided into Britannia Prima and Maxima Caesariensis, with capitals at Cirencester and London respectively, the latter also now being renamed *Augusta*; Britannia Inferior was split into Britannia Secunda and Flavia Caesariensis, with capitals at York and Lincoln.

The death of Constantine in 337 heralded new civil wars and, while these again hardly affected the island directly, they gave the Caledonian Picts and Saxon pirates the confidence to mount a series of attacks on rural Britannia. Then, in 367, they joined forces with the Scots of Hibernia in the 'Great Barbarian Conspiracy', a mass attack introducing a reign of terror across the island. Order was eventually restored by Count Theodosius in 369, and another administrative reorganisation followed, the northern part of Britannia Secunda becoming the province of Valentia, probably with Carlisle as its capital. As such, Valentia seems to have effectively become a military region and was probably where Magnus Maximus, commander of the British army, began his bid for the purple in 383. He stripped the garrison for a march on Rome but was captured at *Aquileia* in 388, after which a new army was sent to Britannia to 'curb the savage Scot and enjoy the lifeless patterns tattooed on dying Picts' (Claudian *B. Gett.* 416–18).

Soon after this episode, however, many of the European provinces began to feel the pressure of attacks by Germanic tribes. Consequently, in 401 Stilicho, Honorius's field marshal, reduced the British garrison in order to defend Italy and Rome itself. This left the British aristocracy in no doubt that the Empire was beginning to fail them and, in 406, they took control of their own destiny. An officer named Marcus was made ruler but, found wanting, was deposed in favour of another military man, Gratian. Four months later, in 407, he too was deposed in favour of Constantine, a soldier of lowly origin, chosen for his name alone. Constantine, however, had much higher ambitions and in 409 took the last of Britannia's regular soldiers with him to march on Rome, leaving a militia in its place. The island once more left open to attack from the Picts, Scots and Saxons, the cities of Britannia denounced him and appealed to Honorius directly for military assistance: the reply was that they should 'look to their own defence', a direct admission that after 366 years Roman rule in the island had ended in all practical senses.

It is against this background that we must interpret the archaeological evidence for the towns of Britannia between the third and fifth centuries. This is particularly true regarding the erection of town defences throughout the island in this period, many of which remain as the most visible evidence for Britain's Roman past. After all, the building of urban fortifications was not only a rarely exercised privilege, one granted only by the emperor, but in the early Roman Empire they were little more than symbolic structures, defining the limits of a community. For this reason, 'defences' existed only at places of high status and were never intended for defence as such, being often little more than ceremonial gateways marking the entrances to the settlement, as with the two archways known at *Verulamium*, defining the limits of the original *municipium*. Quite simply, during the *pax Romana* imperial government saw no need for building truly defensive works at any of the urban centres. Thus when the *colonia* at Colchester was founded, the original legionary defences on the east were destroyed to allow for urban expansion, while those on the west were partly levelled for the building of a triumphal arch to mark both the formal limits of the colony and the conquest of Britannia: consequently, the place was defenceless when Boudicca attacked in AD 60.

The Boudiccan Revolt was probably the reason that defences were erected about that time at Chichester, Silchester and Winchester. These fortifications were little more than palisaded earthen ramparts with a ditch in front, hardly expressions of urban prestige but indicating an urgent need to defend a place against attack by rebels. Likewise, the uncertainty occasioned by the revolt and in its aftermath meant that both *Verulamium* and Colchester were enclosed by earthen fortifications when later rebuilt. Moreover, when the legionary fortresses at Exeter, Lincoln and Gloucester were given over for civilian use in the late first century, the existing military defences were not only kept intact but regularly maintained in good order.

Earth-and-timber fortifications, however, erode and decay, and existing examples were often later repaired or replaced with masonry constructions. By the early second century, for example, the defences at Colchester, Lincoln and Gloucester had all been refurbished and strengthened by the insertion of a narrow stone wall, and their gateways reconstructed in stone. Such work can be explained as demonstrations of municipal prestige, as can the masonry perimeters built at London, Cirencester and Exeter at the beginning of the second century, and the elaborate stone gate-structures built at many other places at this time.

Yet municipal prestige certainly cannot explain why most of the remaining cities and some twenty-five civilian *vici* were enclosed by earthen defences in a rash of activity between 190 and 210, especially as in some cases, as at Silchester and Caistor-by-Norwich, these excluded undeveloped *insulae* peripheral to the main area of urban occupation. Given that the ubiquity of such works is one of the most striking aspects of the towns of Britannia, without parallel in the rest of the Empire at this time, a common foundation date seems more likely, most probably after Albinus stripped the island's garrison in 193–7.

What is perhaps even more surprising is that, once these earthen defences were in place, they remained there to be improved on in later years. The evidence is uneven, but excavations have demonstrated that many were subsequently consolidated by adding a 2–3 metre wide stone wall, although in some cases, as at *Verulamium*, these new masonry defences followed a slightly different circuit from their predecessors (figure 3). That apart, the date of reconstruction clearly varied from place to place. At *Verulamium*, for example, renewal began in c.240, at Silchester it was a decade later, while the riverside wall at London was not built until 270 or so. Dorchester, however, did not renew its fortifications until c.300, while those at Caerwent were not replaced in stone until about 330, and Mildenhall received its masonry defences after 354. We might assume the date of reconstruction depended more on local financial ability than a response to a concerted threat but, even so, the fact that these defences were even retained, never mind restored, suggests a significant degree of lawlessness in the island. After all, the main reason for any fortification is to deter direct assault by an enemy, yet there is no evidence that Britannia was beset by external attackers at this time. Perhaps a combination of regional importance in the administrative scheme and the need for a more effective deterrent to localised bandit raids lay behind their upkeep and subsequent modification.

This being so, an explanation can be suggested for the final and somewhat puzzling adjustment made to many of these urban defences: the addition of projecting towers (for example, plate 15). In a strictly defensive context, these were intended for trained troops to create areas of flanking fire against a massed attack, and it was long thought they were all built in c.369 as part of a reorganisation of Britannia's defences by Count Theodosius. On the other hand, with the exception of London, none of the cities and towns of Britannia ever had a permanent garrison, but instead relied most probably on a local militia for its defence. Moreover, the location of the towers on the individual circuits often shows little real regard for tactical defence, nor were they always added in the consistent way required for systematic crossfire. For example,

Plate 15. A tower on the south defences at Caerwent: the vertical line at the junction of tower and city wall shows it was added at a later date.

Lincoln and Brough-on-Humber excepted, they were rarely built close to gateways, the weakest part of any defensive work, while at Caerwent none was provided on the west and east sides; at *Verulamium* only two such towers seem to have been built, while none at all was added at Silchester. Finally, it is clear that in some places the towers were added before 367, as at Caerwent, where they were built *c*.348–9 (plate 15). From this we might resolve that the decision to add projecting towers was not a response to a specific threat or as part of any military reorganisation but determined by both civic status and a recognition of their deterrent factor against all but the most obstinate of attackers.

Their defences apart, the general picture that emerges from a study of the Roman-British cities and towns is that their public infrastructure radically deteriorated in the late third and fourth centuries. This shift is most obviously seen in how the *basilicae* of several cities evidently lost their original purpose and function about then. That at Silchester, for example, began to be used for metal-working in about 250; those at Wroxeter and London had partially collapsed by 300; and those at

Caerwent and Exeter were systematically demolished between 350 and 375. Similarly, other public facilities at many cities also now began to fall into disuse, the *thermae* at Wroxeter and Canterbury by 330 and 350 respectively, the amphitheatres at London and Cirencester by 350, and the theatre at *Verulamium* by 375, after which it became a rubbish-dump. These events imply a critical if gradual change in the social and political outlook of the communities as a whole, a lack of motivation and resources for their maintenance, local autonomy by now having succumbed to the decisions of imperial officials. They in turn apparently determined that available civic funds be spent on the defences of what were now little more than regional administrative and taxation centres, rather than places which combined political and social facilities and amenities along with a bureaucratic function.

Other archaeological evidence from the towns of Britannia provides even clearer proof for a major transformation in their social nature in the third and fourth centuries. While it would be foolish to adopt a dogmatic view on the basis of very patchy evidence, it seems that at most urban centres industrial and manufacturing activities reached their apogee in the late second century, after which these places acquired more of the nature of a garden city. This is seen most obviously in the plan of most late Roman-British urban residences, which took on the characteristic form of a substantial compound-house, often highly decorated and adorned with mosaics and frescoes, and sometimes with their own private bath-suite (for example, figure 17C and D). Moreover, many of these residential complexes can be associated with agricultural buildings and there is even direct evidence that parts of their compounds were used for agricultural activity and grain-drying and storage. Indeed, it seems that the stimulus for their appearance was a long-term climatic decline that began in about 300–50, as a sustained shorter and wetter growing season lowered crop production, in turn reducing the population by natural means to a lower sustainable level. As such, these urban farms are the ultimate origin of the so-called 'Dark Earth' marking the late-Roman levels at many of the British cities, a soil resulting from sustained agriculture and manuring. It seems the late-Roman cities of Britannia were no different from their equivalents in contemporary Gaul: 'within the gates of the cities, yoked oxen now ploughed furrows, seed was sown, and corn reaped and threshed' (Libanius *Orat.* 18.34–5).

The urban landscape of later Roman Britain, therefore, was dominated by what were effectively urban villas or farms. Their owners were providing their own food, rather than relying on any erratic supplies produced in the countryside; in short, the urban population had reverted to the subsistence economy that prevailed on the island before the

Roman invasion. And here we probably have a final clue for the radical transformation of the late Roman-British cities from what they had been some three hundred years earlier. Britain lacked any form of developed and unified economic and political system at the time of the Roman conquest (see Chapter 1). Thus the Romans had to introduce an urban network, a series of local administrative centres purely for the convenience and requirements of the imperial government. That these centres in turn assumed a fully urbanised identity was made possible only by the desires of their leading citizens, while their localised marketing function and industrial role developed from attracting a large and settled population and a stable economic system. During the second and third centuries, however, local autonomy was gradually removed and the monetary system slowly collapsed. In a society which never became completely monetarised or industrialised, the primary function of these artificial creations was no longer relevant. As the economy geared itself to relying on barter on a purely local scale, with coin of any type or real value becoming increasingly rare, there was even less need for permanent urban communities of any size.

Despite all of these setbacks, as well as the formal cessation of Roman rule in 410, occupation nonetheless continued in many of the urban centres of Britannia well into the fifth century. At *Verulamium*, for example, new buildings were being erected in *c*.410–30; at Wroxeter a sizeable timber-framed building, probably two storeys high, was constructed at about the same time; at Cirencester the *forum* was kept clean until 430 or a little later; and the collapsed roof of a building in London sealed an Anglo-Saxon brooch, suggesting it stood until 450 or later. Such continued urban activity is to be expected: the defences of these cities guaranteed some form of protection against attacks by marauding Saxons and the like, as they became increasingly common in this period. On the other hand, the shortage of manpower for defence meant that many of the 'surplus' gateways at several towns needed to be blocked for better protection against attack (for example, plate 16). But such activity does not indicate that organised town life continued to this date. True, literary evidence informs us that in 429 and again in 440 the religious leaders of the Britons appealed to the Gaulish bishop Germanus for help in combating heretics; but it was the church that made the request, not the urban communities. Likewise, we learn that the native Roman-British aristocracy tenaciously clung to the trappings and titles of organised political life in this period, as did the father of St Patrick, who claimed the rank of *decurion*, while Ambrosius Aurelianus, a mid-fifth-century army commander, was of senatorial rank. Yet the main residences of both were evidently their rural estates.

The simple fact was that, as the urban centres no longer had any

Plate 16. The blocked south gate of Caerwent: note the drain opening at the bottom.

political, economic or social purpose, they had become little more than defended centres with a small resident population. Even so, as has been proved at so many excavations, all the urban centres of Britannia were abandoned by *c*.500, and none was reoccupied until some two hundred years later. Why this was so will never be certainly known, but a likely explanation is provided by the climatic decline which began in the fourth century, and the series of pandemics which affected large areas of western Europe in the early fifth. The effect of the first not only reduced the urban population but left the malnourished survivors vulnerable to ailments. A highly infectious disease, like the recorded pandemic of 443 – whether scarlet fever, smallpox or influenza – would devastate a poorly nurtured society lacking modern medicines. (It is salutary to note that 58 per cent of the 168,000 fatalities in the Crimean War were from diseases such as cholera, while some 20 million died in the Spanish flu epidemic of 1918–21, twice the total killed in action during all four years of the First World War.) Evidence for a possible pandemic in late Roman Britain may be the unburied bodies found lying by main roads in Cirencester in mid-fifth-century contexts.

We might therefore visualise a process in which a long-term series of economic and climatic processes, and short-term episodes of virulent disease, resulted in a gradual depopulation of the urban centres and a growing inability to defend them. In 446, as 'a dread and infamous famine gripped the Britons … and deadly plague pressed on the people' (Gildas *Exc. Brit.* 20 and 22), the Saxons, Picts and Scots increased their attacks, and a futile appeal for help was sent to Aetius, commander of Rome. It was the last gasp of a 'Roman' Britain for, as we learn from Bede, when the Saxons returned in strength in 449 it was as settlers not raiders, beginning the Anglicisation of England. They migrated to the island knowing that there was no risk of organised resistance and that they could settle where they wanted. A few lived briefly in some of the semi-deserted cities, such as Canterbury, Colchester and Winchester, where sunken huts of characteristic Saxon type and of mid-fifth-century date are cut into deposits over ruined Roman buildings (figure 22B). In general, however, the overall pattern of early Anglo-Saxon settlement shows a marked tendency to avoid such places, most likely because of the strongly rural tradition of these Germanic peoples, favouring small dispersed settlements over larger nucleated ones; but also, perhaps, because of a natural tendency to shun places of decay, disease and death.

The ruined cities instead became emblematic of the immutable process of decline inherent in the natural world. As an eighth-century poet noted of an unknown place (possibly Bath), it was once

> A city graced with buildings, and many bath-houses;
> Strewn with high peaked gables, and many great warriors;
> And many mead-halls, all filled with revellers.
> Fate changed all that: as it shall ever be. (*The Ruin*, 21–4)

Our anonymous poet believed he lived in the final age of the world, symbolised by the decay of powerful cities and empires, and held he was marking time before the coming of the Kingdom of God. In fact he was marking the genesis of an entirely new and distinct culture. By his time, what was Britannia had become 'Angleland'; Latin was used on a regular basis only – and badly at that – by members of the church, for Saxon had become the vernacular; Roman laws and institutions had been mainly replaced by Germanic traditions. In Wales and Cornwall, however, the parts of Britain never fully urbanised in the Roman period, British Celtic continued as the principal language, and certain Roman laws were maintained. In Caledonia, on the other hand, an area never Romanised to any great extent, the immigrant Scots were busy imposing their own quite different Celtic dialect, and political and legal systems.

This was the real impact of the Anglo-Saxon conquest. 'Angleland', formed from the most Romanised part of Britain, became the only one of Rome's western territories to be fully transformed into a barbarian kingdom, a process so complete that it created a state of insularity that still conditions English attitudes today.

8
Further reading

This bibliography is for the reader who wants more information about the urban framework of Roman Britain and the various topics covered in this survey. The list is not comprehensive, and avoids site-specific monographs, but does include those books which have been found most useful during undergraduate-level teaching: references to other more specialised works will be found in each of them. In addition, regular accounts of excavations in Roman-British towns are to be found in *Britannia*, an annual journal published by the Society for the Promotion of Roman Studies, Senate House, Malet Street, London WC1E 7HU.

Alcock, J.P. *Life in Roman Britain*. Batsford, 1996.
Allason-Jones, L. *Women in Roman Britain*. British Museum Publications, 1989.
Allen, D. *Roman Glass in Britain*. Shire, 1998.
de la Bédoyère, G. *Samian Ware*. Shire, 1988.
de la Bédoyère, G. *The Buildings of Roman Britain*. Batsford, 1991.
de la Bédoyère, G. *Roman Towns in Britain*. Batsford, 1992.
de la Bédoyère, G. *The Golden Age of Roman Britain*. Tempus, 1999.
de la Bédoyère, G. *Pottery in Roman Britain*. Shire, 2000.
Birley, A.R. *The People of Roman Britain*. Batsford, 1979.
Birley, A.R. *The Fasti of Roman Britain*. Clarendon, 1981.
Brown, A.E. *Roman Small Towns in Eastern England and Beyond*. Oxbow, 1995.
Burnham, B., and Wacher, J.S. *The Small Towns of Roman Britain*. Batsford, 1990.
Dark, K. and P. *The Landscape of Roman Britain*. Sutton, 1997.
Frere, S.S. *Britannia*. Pimlico, 1991.
Green, M. *The Gods of Roman Britain*. Shire, 1983; reprinted 1994.
Greene, K. *The Archaeology of the Roman Economy*. Routledge, 1990.
Hanley, R. *Villages in Roman Britain*. Shire, second edition 2000.
Henig, M. *Religion in Roman Britain*. Batsford, 1984.
Ireland, S. *Roman Britain: a Sourcebook*. Croom Helm, 1986.
Johnson, P. *Romano-British Mosaics*. Shire, second edition 1987; reprinted 1995.
Johnson, S. *Later Roman Britain*. Routledge, 1980.
Jones, G.B.D., and Mattingley, D. *An Atlas of Roman Britain*. Blackwell, 1990.
Jones, M. *The End of Roman Britain*. Cornell, 1996.
Ling, R. *Romano-British Wall Painting*. Shire, 1985.

McLeavy, T. *Life in Roman Britain*. English Heritage, 1999.

McWhirr, A.D. *Roman Crafts and Industries*. Shire, 1982; reprinted 1988.

Millet, M. *The Romanization of Britain*. Cambridge, 1990.

Millet, M. *The English Heritage Book of Roman Britain*. Batsford, 1995.

Niblett, R. *Verulamium – The Roman City of St Albans*. Tempus, 2001.

Ordnance Survey. *Map and Guide to Roman Britain*. Ordnance Survey, 1995.

Ottoway, P. *A Traveller's Guide to Roman Britain*. Routledge, 1987.

Potter, T.W., and Johns, C. *Roman Britain*. British Museum Press, 1992.

Rivet, A.L., and Smith, C. *The Place-Names of Roman Britain*. Batsford, 1979.

Rook, T. *Roman Baths in Britain*. Shire, 1992.

Salway, P. *The Oxford Illustrated History of Roman Britain*. Clarendon, 1993.

Salway, P. *A History of Roman Britain*. Clarendon, 1997.

Wacher, J.S. *The Towns of Roman Britain*. Routledge, 1995.

Wacher, J.S. *Roman Britain*. Sutton, 1998.

Wilson, R.J.A. *A Guide to the Roman Remains in Britain*. Constable, third edition 1999.

9
Sites and museums to visit

Aldborough: defences and building remains with mosaics.

Bath: *Roman Baths Museum and Pump Room*, Bath, Somerset BA1 1LZ. Telephone: 01225 477774. Website: www.romanbaths.co.uk

Bristol: *City Museum and Art Gallery*, Queen's Road, Bristol BS8 1RL. Telephone: 0117 922 3571. Website: www.bristol-city.gov.uk (Material from Sea Mills.)

Caerwent: defences; Roman house; Romano-Celtic temple.

Caistor-by-Norwich: defences.

Canterbury: defences (St Mary Northgate); theatre (Slatters, St Mary Northgate Street); St Martin's Church (*martyrium?*); *Royal Museum and Art Gallery*, 18 High Street, Canterbury, Kent. Telephone: 01227 452747. Website: www.canterbury-museum.co.uk

Cardiff: *National Museum of Wales*, Cathays Park, Cardiff CF10 3NP. Telephone: 029 2039 7951. Website: www.nmgw.ac.uk

Carlisle: *Tullie House Museum and Art Gallery*, Castle Street, Carlisle, Cumbria CA3 8TP. Telephone: 01228 534781.

Carmarthen: amphitheatre (Priory Close); *Carmarthenshire County Museum*, Abergwili, Carmarthen, Carmarthenshire SA31 2JQ. Telephone: 01267 231691. Website: www.carmarthenshire.gov.uk

Chester: legionary amphitheatre; *Grosvenor Museum*, 27 Grosvenor Street, Chester CH1 2DD. Telephone: 01244 402008. Website: www.chestercc.gov.uk

Chichester: amphitheatre (Whyke Lane); *Chichester District Museum*, 29 Little London, Chichester, West Sussex PO19 1PB. Telephone: 01243 784683.

Cirencester: defences (London Road); amphitheatre (Martin Close); *Corinium Museum*, Park Street, Cirencester, Gloucestershire GL7 2BX. Telephone: 01285 655611. Website: www.cotswold.gov.uk (Reconstructed Roman rooms.)

Colchester: Balkerne Gate; Butt Road church; *Castle Museum*, Castle Park, Colchester, Essex CO1 1TJ. Telephone: 01206 282939. (Temple vaults beneath.)

Corbridge: remains of military and civil buildings, including temples; *Corbridge Roman Site Museum*, Corbridge, Northumberland NE45 5NT. Telephone: 01434 632349. Website: www.english-heritage.org.uk

Dorchester: Colliton Park Roman House; Maumbury Rings amphitheatre; aqueduct (Poundbury Camp); *Dorchester County Museum*, High West Street, Dorchester, Dorset DT1 1XA. Telephone: 01305 262735. Website: www.dorset.museum.clara.net

Dover: The Roman Painted House, New Street, Dover CT17 9AJ. Telephone: 01304 203279. Website: www.geocities.com/anthro-arch/RPH.html

Exeter: defences (Northernhay Gardens and Southernhay); *Royal Albert*

Memorial Museum, Queen Street, Exeter EX4 3RX. Telephone: 01392 665858. Website: www.exeter.gov.uk

Gloucester: east gate (Boots, Eastgate Street); defences (King's Walk); *City Museum and Art Gallery*, Brunswick Road, Gloucester GL1 1HP. Telephone: 01452 524131.

Leicester: Jewry Wall (*thermae*); *Jewry Wall Museum and Site*, St Nicholas Circle, Leicester LE1 4LB. Telephone: 0116 247 3021. Website: www.leicestermuseums.ac.uk

Lincoln: Newport Arch; east gate (Eastgate Hotel); lower west gate (Orchard Street); Mint Wall (*basilica*, Castle Hotel); *City and County Museum*, 12 Friars Lane, Lincoln LN2 5AL. Telephone: 01522 530401.

London: Temple of Mithras (rebuilt in Temple Court); Roman building (Lower Thames Street – by appointment with Museum of London); defences (London Wall, Tower Hill and Cooper's Row). *The British Museum* (Great Russell Street, London WC1B 3DG; telephone: 020 7636 1555; website: www.thebritishmuseum.ac.uk) has much London material, but see also the *Museum of London* (London Wall, London EC2Y 5HN; telephone: 020 7600 3699; website: www.museum-london.org.uk), which has excellent displays and reconstructed Roman rooms.

Newcastle upon Tyne: *The Museum of Antiquities*, University of Newcastle upon Tyne, Newcastle upon Tyne NE1 7RU. Telephone: 0191 222 7846 or 7849. Website: www.ncl.ac.uk/~nantiq

Newport: *Newport Museum and Art Gallery*, John Frost Square, Newport, Gwent NP9 1PA. Telephone: 01633 840064. (Material from Caerwent.)

Reading: *Museum of Reading*, The Town Hall, Blagrave Street, Reading RG1 1QH. Telephone: 0118 939 9800. Website: www.readingmuseum.org (Material from Silchester.)

Sea Mills, Bristol: Portway Roman House.

Shrewsbury: *Shrewsbury Museum and Art Gallery* (Rowley's House), Barker Street, Shrewsbury, Shropshire SY1 1QH. Telephone: 01743 361196. Website: www.shrewsburymuseums.com (Material from Wroxeter.)

Silchester: defences; amphitheatre; *Calleva Museum*, The Rectory, Bramley Road, Silchester, Reading RG7 2LU. Telephone: 0118 970 0825.

Verulamium: theatre; parts of several buildings; defences; *Verulamium Museum*, St Michaels, St Albans, Hertfordshire AL3 4SW. Telephone: 01727 751810. Website: www.stalbansmuseum.org.uk

Wall: *mansio*; *balneum*; *Wall Roman Site and Museum*, Watling Street, Wall, near Lichfield, Staffordshire WS14 0AW. Telephone: 01543 480768. Website: www.english-heritage.org.uk

Wroxeter: The Old Work (*thermae*); *forum* colonnade; *macellum*; *Wroxeter Roman City*, Wroxeter Roman Site, Wroxeter, Shropshire SY5 6PH. Telephone: 01743 761330.

York: *The Yorkshire Museum*, Museum Gardens, York YO1 7FR. Telephone: 01904 551800. Website: www.york.gov.uk

10
Roman names of some places mentioned in the text

Modern name: *Roman name*; probable meaning.

Aldborough: *Isurum Brigantum*; (?) of the Brigantes.
Bath: *Aquae Sulis*; spa of Sulis.
Brough-on-Humber: *Petuaria*; (?).
Buxton: *Aquae Arnemetiae*; spa at shrine of Ar … (?).
Caerwent: *Venta Silurum*; market of the Silures.
Caistor-by-Norwich: *Venta Icenorum*; market of the Iceni.
Canterbury: *Durovernum Cantiacorum*; fort at the marsh of the Cantii.
Carlisle: *Luguvalium*; Lugos's strong fort.
Carmarthen: *Moridunum Demetarum*; Morius's fort of the Demetae.
Catterick: *Cataractonium*; at the waterfalls.
Chelmsford: *Caesaromagus*; Caesar's market.
Chester: *Deva*; (?).
Chichester: *Noviomagus Reginorum*; new market of the Regini.
Cirencester: *Corinium Dobunnorum*; (?) of the Dobunni.
Colchester: *Camulodunum / Colonia Claudia Victricensis*; fortress of Camulos / Claudius victory colony.
Corbridge: *Coriostopitum*; (?) of the Corio (?).
Dorchester: *Durnovaria (Durotrigum)*; place of 'fist-sized' pebbles (of the Durotriges).
Exeter: *Isca Dumnoniorum*; (?) of the Dumnonii.
Gloucester: *Glevum / Colonia Nervia Glevenis*; famous place / Nerva's colony at Glevum.
Ilchester: *Lindinis*; the marsh.
Leicester: *Ratae Corieltavorum*; fortification of the Corieltavi.
Lincoln: *Lindum/Colonia (Domitiana) Lindenensis*; at the lake / (Domitian's) colony at Lindum.
London: *Londinium/Augusta*; (?) the marshy place / the noble place.
Sea Mills: *Abona*; on the (river) Avon.
Silchester: *Calleva Atrebatum*; the grove of the Atrebates.
Wall: *Letocetum*; (?).
Water Newton: *Durobrivae*; (?) stony place of Brivas.
Winchester: *Venta Belgarum*; market of the Belgae.
Wroxeter: *Viriconium Cornoviorum*; the place of Virico of the Cornovii.
York: *Eburacum / Colonia Eboracensium*; the yew grove / colony at *Eburacum*.

Index

Aediles 15
Ager publicus 9, 29
Ager vectigalis 9, 12
Agriculture 38, 69
Alcester 44, 62
Aldborough 16, 76, 78
Amphitheatres 13, 25, 26, 40, 69, 76, 77
Amphorae 10, 40, 49
Ancaster 28
Aqueducts 21, 22, 76
Arches 27, 48, 66
Bakers 44
Balneum 20, 77
Barley-wine 42
Bartlow 60
Basilica 8, 11, 13, 18, 19, 43, 48, 49, 51, 68, 78
Bath 15, 43, 44, 48, 49, 57, 72, 78
Bath-houses – see *Balneum*; *Thermae*
Bede 72
Beer 42
Binchester 59
Bristol 76
Britannia Inferior 64, 65
Britannia Prima 65
Britannia Secunda 65
Britannia Superior 64, 65
British rulers and officials: Ambrosius Aurelianus 70; Boudicca 11, 29, 37, 46, 56, 57, 66; Cartimandua 9; Cogidubnus 9, 48; Gildas 58, 72; Prausutagus 9, 57
Brooches 43, 70
Brough-on-Humber 15, 16, 26, 39, 44, 68, 78
Buxton 49, 78
Caerleon 15, 35, 54
Caerwent 6, 12, 15, 18, 20, 27, 31, 33, 34, 35, 50, 51, 57, 67, 68, 69, 71, 76, 77, 78
Caistor-by-Norwich 6, 26, 39, 43, 45, 67, 76, 78
Camerton 44
Canterbury 25, 26, 44, 53, 55, 63, 69, 72, 76, 78
Cardiff 76

Carlisle 16, 62, 65, 76, 78
Carmarthen 16, 26, 76, 78
Castellum divisiorum 21
Castleford 43
Catterick 78
Cattle 38, 41
Cellars 32
Celtic languages 58, 72
Censitor 57
Ceramics – *see* Pottery
Cereals 38, 39, 41, 69
Charterhouse 15, 39, 40
Chelmsford 39, 78
Chester 76, 78
Chichester 6, 26, 43, 44, 48, 61, 66, 76, 78
Christianity 47, 52-5, 61, 64
Church Brough 43
Churches 52, 53, 54, 55, 72, 76
Cirencester 6, 12, 15, 26, 43, 44, 56, 62, 65, 66, 69, 70, 71, 76, 78
Civitates 5, 12, 15, 16, 18, 29, 38, 39, 44, 45, 47, 48, 49
Coins 43, 60
Colchester 6, 8, 9, 26, 27, 28, 29, 35, 37, 43, 47, 48, 53, 54, 56, 57, 61, 66, 72, 76, 78
Coloniae 5, 9, 10, 19, 27, 29, 30, 35, 47, 64, 66, 78
Compound-house 33, 34, 35, 69
Conventus 11
Copper 39, 43
Corbridge 16, 48, 78
Courtyard-house 33, 35
Cremations 60, 61
Curator 16
Cursus publicus 20
Dark Earth 69
Death and burial 60-3
Decuriones 9, 12, 70
Defences 48, 66-8, 76, 77
Disease, illnesses, injuries 62, 71
Dolaucothi 39
Dorchester 16, 21, 26, 27, 33, 34, 44, 55, 61, 62, 67, 76, 78

Dover 76
Drains 22
Dried fruits 40
Druids 47
Duoviri 10, 18
Economy 38
Emperors, British: Allectus 65; Carausius 65; Clodius Albinus 64, 67; Constantine 65; Gratian 65; Magnus Maximus 65; Marcus 65
Emperors, Roman: Augustus 47, 64; Domitian 58; Caracalla 64; Claudius 7, 12, 27, 28, 48, 78; Commodus 64; Constantine 65; Decius 54; Diocletian 42, 54, 65; Domitian 78; Galerius 54; Hadrian 15, 16, 27, 46; Honorius 65, 66; Nero 38, 46; Nerva 78; Theodosius 47; Trajan 16, 46, 57; Septimius Severus 64; Severus Alexander 65; Vespasian 22
Exeter 66, 69, 76, 78
Farms 12, 38, 69
Flavia Caesariensis 65
Florus 57
Forum 8, 11, 13, 18, 19, 20, 27, 43, 48, 49, 51, 70
Fountains 21
Frescoes 36, 69
Furniture 36, 37
Garum 40
Germanus, St 70
Gladiators 26, 59
Glass 36, 40, 43, 60
Gloucester 6, 9, 15, 27, 29, 35, 44, 63, 66, 77, 78
Gods: native 49; oriental 51-2; Roman 48, 58
Gold 38, 39, 43
Governor 7, 12, 17, 56, 57
Graffiti, writing 58, 59
Grave-goods 60-1
Greek 57, 58
Greta Bridge 31
Hadrian's Wall 57
Hides, leather 38, 41, 60

Housesteads 14, 63
Hunting-dogs 38, 41
Hypocaust 22, 36
Hypogeum 61
Ilchester 15, 16, 78
Imperial cult 47
Industries 39, 43, 44, 69
Inhumations 60, 61
Insulae 8, 11, 14, 29, 30, 32, 49, 67
Iron 38, 39, 43
Iugera 9
Jews, Judaism 47, 52
Latin 58, 59, 72
Latrines 19, 22
Lead 39, 44, 62
Legatus iuridicius 57
Leicester 12, 19, 21, 22, 23, 24, 26, 36, 43, 44, 59, 77, 78
Lex coloniae 9
Lighting 37, 43
Lincoln 6, 9, 21, 27, 29, 43, 54, 65, 66, 68, 77, 78
London 6, 11, 17, 25, 26, 27, 28, 29, 30, 32, 35, 41, 42, 43, 44, 45, 48, 54, 56, 57, 59, 61, 62, 64, 65, 66, 67, 68, 69, 70, 77, 78
Macella 11, 19, 20, 43, 77
Malton 43
Mansiones 13, 14, 20, 21, 25, 78
Martyria, martyrs 54, 55, 76
Masons, sculptors 43, 57
Maxima Caesariensis 65
Mildenhall 67
Millstones 44
Mithras, Mithraism 51-2, 64, 77
Mosaics 36, 44, 69, 76
Municipia 5, 10, 47, 48, 66
Nettleton Scrub 44, 49
Newcastle upon Tyne 77
Newport 77
Nymphaea 22
Old Carlisle 15
Olives, olive oil 40, 59
Oppida 5, 8, 10
Ordo 9, 10, 12, 15, 19
Oxford 41, 44
Patrick, St 70
Paul, St 52, 57

Pax Romana 19, 66
Pearls 38
Pewter 44, 62
Pharmacists 59
Pottery 40, 41, 43, 44, 45, 60
Poundbury 55, 61
Procurator 56
Provincia 7
Provincial council 7, 47
Quaestores 10
Radishes 42
Reading 77
Respublica 8, 11, 12, 16
Rochester 6
Roman officials: Aetius 72; Agricola, Gn Julius 12, 17, 19, 56, 57; Bassus, Gn Munatius 9, 57; Classicianus, G Julius Alpinus 57; Constantius 38, 65; Decianus Catus 57; Paulinus, Suetonius 57; Paulinus, Ti Claudius 12, 27; Priscus, G Octavius Iavolenus 57; Stilicho 65; Theodosius, Count 65, 67
Rome 7, 9, 10, 12, 39, 46, 47, 53, 57, 65, 72
St Albans 5, 55
Salt 41
Sarcophagi 61
Saxons 65, 70, 72
Scots 65, 72
Sea Mills 14, 15, 41, 63, 76, 77, 78
Senators 7, 39, 57, 70
Seneca 25, 29, 38
Seviri Augustales 47
Shops 29, 43
Shrewsbury 77
Silchester 6, 12, 13, 17, 20, 21, 22, 23, 26, 31, 43, 44, 49, 59, 66, 67, 68, 77, 78
Silver 38, 39, 43, 44, 46, 64
Skeletons 37, 61, 62, 63
Slaves 38, 41
Stadia 25, 27
Stevenage 60
Strabo 7, 38, 45
Strip-house 30, 31, 32, 34, 43
Surgery, surgeons 62-3
Taplow 57

Teachers 57, 58
Temples 8, 17, 47, 48, 49, 50, 51, 76
Territoria 9, 12, 56
Theatres 8, 11, 25, 26, 39, 69, 76, 77
Thermae 22, 23, 24, 25, 69, 77
Tin 39, 44
Tombstones 60
Trade, traders 11, 18, 40, 43
Tribes: Anavionenses 57; Atrebates 12, 13, 78; Belgae 78; Brigantes 9, 15, 78; Cantii 78; Carvetti 16; Catuvellauni 10; Corieltavi 12, 78; Corionototae 16; Cornovii 78; Dematae 16, 78; Dobunni 16, 78; Dumnonii 78; Durotrages 16, 78; Iceni 9, 39, 78; Parisii 16; Picts 65, 72; Regini 9, 48, 78; Silures 12, 78
Tributa 7, 28, 39, 57
Valentia 65
Verulamium 5, 6, 10, 11, 18, 19, 25, 26, 29, 30, 32, 36, 43, 44, 48, 54, 56, 66, 67, 68, 69, 70, 77
Vici 5, 13, 14, 15, 16, 25, 31, 39, 43, 45, 48, 54, 56, 63, 67
Villas 12, 39, 45, 53, 69; Frampton 53; Hinton St Mary 53; Lullingstone 53
Wall 20, 77, 78
Water Newton 6, 14, 41, 44, 45, 54, 59, 78
Weston under Penyard 15
Winchester 6, 42, 44, 61, 66, 72, 78
Wine 40, 42
Wool 42
Wroxeter 6, 19, 20, 23, 43, 44, 48, 56, 68, 69, 70, 77, 78
York 15, 27, 28, 35, 43, 52, 54, 58, 60, 61, 62, 64, 65, 77, 78